INDIOM

indiom

Daljit Nagra

faber

First published in 2023
by Faber & Faber Ltd
The Bindery, 51 Hatton Garden
London EC1N 8HN

Typeset by Hamish Ironside
Printed in the UK by TJ Books Limited, Padstow, Cornwall

A CIP record for this book is available from the British Library

ISBN 978-0-571-37225-6

FSC
www.fsc.org
MIX
Paper from
responsible sources
FSC® C013056

Printed and bound in the UK on FSC® certified paper in line with our continuing
commitment to ethical business practices, sustainability and the environment.
For further information see faber.co.uk/environmental-policy

2 4 6 8 10 9 7 5 3 1

Contentment of Shot List

◄I§N√T»E¿R♥M■IʃSiS✱I∧OꟍN☉~

Dramatis Personae

Addendum: CHORUS is performed by 50 hijras, third gender, who often speak simultaneously, in deference to the original Greek CHORUS

CANTO I

CANTO I

Prologue by Screenwriter's Companion

PROLOGUE on Babus & Coolie languages, & how
Nissim Ezekiel's poem *Goodbye Party for Miss Push-
pa T.S.*, written in Babu English, caused offence on
publication in 1970s India

Screenwriter's Companion lowers a book & speaks into the camera

Salutations. Hi, I'm sat by greenwood tree in kameez
& jodhpur. I'm sate as Ms Barrett Browning who once say,
she eat, she drink so much of classics from under a tree,
        so much that her head ache!

In this break from my 'eat & drink', our screenwriter ask for ars
poetica to announce her talkie, aka film.
They said, to disclose the gist that might aid the baat – the yarn,
        but in Standard English.

Screenwriter's Companion gulps at the thought of attempting Standard English

But first, I'd mention the Victorians who sought civil
servants to run the Raj – these were Babus; the Coolie was
the skivvy. Today's talkie imagines how their English
        endures in modern verse.

I'm sure you'd also adore knowhow of some lingo terms.
Indioms flow from the mood engagement between English
& Indian. Babu & Coolie are both indioms.
        Babu is eccentric

use of indioms. So high Babu is a lavish play
for least 'actual' speech. Meanwhile, Coolie's an oral record
from the unschooled, & low mix of indioms may embrace
        excessive Indic words.

Screenwriter's Companion raises their script, clears the throat
then recites an 'ars poetica'

Monthly poetry groups flourish over world giving best
counsel, inspiration & samosa. Today's writing
group, in March 2020, is no different except
        the hill station setting –

is it in India? These Indic-heritage poets,
of whom but-not-one earn their crust in Ind, gather monthly
from over the globe. This month, they're in Bulbul Hall,
    which sits
        in the vale – Charsovee.

Today's theme is about a poem published five decade
distant by our 'Englisch Langwidge' poet from Ind, Mr
Nissim Ezekiel, you know him? P.S. quote was made
        by that great pretender

Mr Pound, of Mr Eliot's *Wasteland*. Nissim's lay
was for a fellow of his committee – she was leaving,
back in '70s, for good. Sad story? The lay was gay!
        Beaming Babu English.

'Badmash – his new poem! Is, he think, how we perorate!?'
It's how most felt mocked while sat under punkah, including
the lass in his lines! Today's poets will assess the fate
        of all such corruptings.

Oh so exciting! Will they go cut-throat barrack for high
drama in defence of Babu verse, or troop for groupthink;
a porcupine's test – get close as a hug till the pricks bite
          or, 'let's hold back for quilled

stimulus – we're comrades in one individual soul'.
Furthermore, as I've said, Babus were administrators
nurtured by men from the Atlantic Archipelago.
          These sahibs were masters

of the Babu, the Babu in turn mastered the Coolie.
Dear viewer, to add, please put aside your traditional
& classically trained methods. Our sensibility's
          an odd conceptual

double-helixing of the houses where we take our lease.
Plus our polymaths weren't groomed to speak but to execute
paperwork assisting the Raj. Now if you won't mind, please,
          while young Bodleian dude

sits in the Bodleian – I'll stay out here under greenwood
with this spicy-red book. What is it – is an Indian
elementary reader designed for the use of stud-
          ents in the Anglo-vern

acular school, published in 1877,
writ by Mr A. Woollaston, who famously lobby
against vaccines. His book's not apropos to what you'll learn;
          now, go – watch talkie!

Cameras recede as Screenwriter's Companion continues speaking

Before you go, I'll recite from the primer, but please note
those in heavenly situ often recite back-to-front.

Just for you, I'll recite in the de-rigueur mortal mode
    for a moral once taught.

Screenwriter's Companion recites from the primer

Politeness

An officer in battle happening to stoop his head, a cannon-ball passed completely over it & took off the head of a soldier who stood behind him. 'You see,' said the officer, 'that a man never loses by politeness.' Anon.

Screenwriter's Companion raises a finger & summons the cameras back

Additional addendum. Are Babus ever modest?
Swell show offs we are for certs always offloading info!
Do not be set off course, but keep pace with our exchanges.
    Onward Christian pongos!

2

Mr Desani's welcoming speech

On the theme of the poetry workshop – to write in
Babu or in Standard English, & the politics of speak-
ing in an Indian accent

Director & Camera Operator are seen in the top left corner of Bulbul Hall

Director says to Camera Operator:
Pulley curtains apart – this talkie's operative.
Poets are inhabited to the swing
of the new environ. They're cushy seated.

Camera Operator replies:
We're quids-in for Mr Vishnoodas!
Staring out he is from this valley
of Charsovee. His timbre gives brass-
in-pocket feeling. Lo! Our swami!

Director whispers:
Focus on his teeth – they're seaside-bright
despiting air in Ind's interjected with grit.

Camera Operator whispers:
Mr Vishnoodas Desani is don a polka bow tie
for aide-memoiring Mr D. Thomas, the Divine
Clown. Mr Vishnoodas has raise a folio.

Director whispers:
It's a lay by Mr Nissim Ezekiel – he's our first to
write, albeit a few poems, in the style of Babu.

Camera Operator refers to Mr Desani:
So cheeky – he's recite to himself from his hardback
Collected Poems, this *Goodbye Party for Miss Pushpa
T.S.* in thick Indian accent! He's harvesting a laugh.

Mr Desani recites two extracts from Nissim Ezekiel's
Goodbye Party for Miss Pushpa T.S., *which is written in low Babu
(very close to modern Indian-English)*

Mr Desani mumbling to himself:
Friends,
our dear sister
is departing for foreign
in two three days,
&
we are meeting today
to wish her bon voyage

Whenever I asked her to do anything,
she was saying, 'Just now only
I will do it.' That is showing
good spirit.

Camera Operator whispers to Director:
The Babu aspects of Mr Ezekiel's lay –
how will our audience appreciate?

Director whispers:
Must be darn patient to be watching *indiom*.
They will appreciate the Babu in that quotation –

its French usage, its hugger-mugger syntax,
& 'two three' being specific to Anglo-Indic chat.

*Mr Desani lowers the book & looks at the poets around the workshop table
which seems to be set in a room reminiscent of a drawing by M. C. Escher*

Mr Vishnoodas Desani says to all:
Hail all committee, muses et cetera – Council must
take arms against the dulce et decorum of conflicts –
to blot onwards in pure English or rage for indioms.

No Dionysian theatre this month, like nabobs instead
let's judge from this discombobulate floor. Our multitude
seating's topsy-turvy – I feel dunked in a pit while you

seem boxed or galleried. I say, we're helicopterised
swaying in this hall that Mr Escher may have designed,
a hall Mr Daedalus or Da Vinci had dome-dreamed.

Yet we poets are here, realised in its wooded five
dimensions. To walk this way is to seem stepped down a
    flight,
walk that way & seem on a wall – this Everest-to-ant

perspective in a solo look. Look outside – oh peak of
Ind winking nether at the docked Chandrayaan, our rocket
that slaked the lunar waters while NASA looked on wilted.

Oh Ind, from this hill – what cottages weep panegyrics
to their siblings in Wessex, plus Walden. Yonder, what pokes
through those groves – a Victorian bookstore with folios

hot pressed by Graywolf, Bloodaxe or Black Inc, in Oz,
    heaped fresh,

fresher than the shelves at Hay. Hail! Our destinies are fissured – mine soul follows Nissim, mine nut flows aft Percy
  Bysshe.

*Cameras have suddenly turned to focus on Director (unknown to Director
& Camera Operator) which will be the case throughout the talkie although
both these men will remain unaware that they're being filmed*

    Director whispers to Camera Operator:
He parleys in fixed syllables, made suave
by a pivot rhyme, an $A = A / B = B$ weave.

    Camera Operator replies:
I'm hearing full & perfect triple rhyme.
He's our great vowel shifter – our bi-
bender of the consonant. Hai! –

    Director takes charge:
Mr Desani – be back at him,
he's vaping up a brain of steam.

Mr Desani is seen & heard again addressing the poets around the table

Well zoomed for voluntary displacement, parishioners,
some from nearby vale, some from Motherland, having
  traversed
like Jane Austen's man of many vehicles, Mr Clifford –

you may have come by chariot, chaise, landeau, landeaulet,
by phaeton, gig, whiskey, curricle, teleport, by jet
or wheelbarrow. By whatever means – let me end my jest

by returning us to the oracle of the parping
tuk-tuk of a day Nissim performed before Miss Pushpa,
in the 1970s, an au revoir in Babu,

in her own voice to recall our Indic 'noise' in the Raj.
Ho! Babu – our conjugal cake of anglophones, our marz-
ipan juggernaut with which we mela our poetic muse.

Persian was replaced by English, for Queen Victoria,
for our knee salute & clerical charge in white collar.
English was never for us an hors d'oeuvres & colloquy;

happy keeping Sahib's books, hoc est broke verbum meum,
happy with hand by heart quoting Homer's encomium
in phonetics that rougèd the lugs of Dr Johnson.

Our reward? We became bud-buds from Kipling to Orwell
onward to Rushdie. Prat-fall Babus! How do we repel
this sowing of the purse so pockets of scorn do not reap?

Does our language of resistance sound queer as a clockwork
orange, a stitch in canonical time that's holding on
with empire wound – are we the musical of Frankenstein?

All I can say, our national tree has limbs bountiful
willy-nilly brewing foetus who are wide-mawed, reared tall
in Coolie or Babu. Does English breed – by our windfall!

Cameras have been distracted by Director
while Mr Desani continues speaking

Director whispers to Camera Operator:
For those seeking to read the script
of our talkie, I say – they're welcome to recite
in an Indian accent. Particularly if they can
ensure there is zero separation between
self & the accent. To do this, they must embody
our auburn delivery with requisite humility.

Camera Operator tries to clarify the idea:
If accent's a horse the speaker feel they're riding
for fun – such riding becomes deriding.

Director replies:
In sooth, who could ever imitate your accent,
its biryani of Wiltshire-to-Indian
plus Canadian from your years in Newfoundland.

Camera Operator, smiling, replies:
Newfie! A sleeveen I am. But let me suggest,
if reader cannot create our complex accents
from this folio – what worth the writ version.

Director changes the subject:
Our troubadours must be more phlegm & clement.
Some swing doolally in their seat of settlement.

Camera Operator whispers:
Mr Vishnoodas is his own bel esprit! How his head
it fall then jut like a turban warrior to duplicate
our bombasticated guru – Henry at Agincourt!
Who would mock the mixed metaphors, the pan-
jandrum of jollity Mr Desani is use. The manner
by which he is sending himself up is a gentle
teasing of our beloved lingo. Look how he handle
the scimitar peaks of his imperial moustachio –
each blade add to the arc as he charge for his coda.

*Cameras turn to Mr Desani who is now standing
while addressing his fellow poets*

Our windfall abounds! I say it is here with my yellow
crossed garters, with the camera crew decked in pink dayglow,

with our Clee Hills, there, where Shropshire lads are buried
   & hope

for rebirth in our Babu tongue! I can no more compos
mentis far-off Bodo Babu than Coolie Telugus
hawking. Each mulligatawny is a milieu music.

All hail, muse! I have unpicnic'd the gingham of the grass,
the grass – see how it grows long-haired over the stiff aggros
of its squared lawn. What if we skirt past Nissim for Oxo-

nian's franchised flavour, must we bear Babu in secret
on the spine down to Pandæmonium? To strive, to seek
summum bonums, the golden chain of Homer so we speak

for sheer bananas, when we become again guerrilla
poets, diablo's rabble, gondoliering militia!
So let's try to listen now, to hear each parishioner

defend or damn Nissim's Babu. What if he were with us
now, would he Dunciad himself with, *oops, so sorry Miss
Pushpa*, or fashionista her in Babu till she's beaming?

     Camera turns to Director & Camera Operator

    Director whispers to Camera Operator:
I admire your short fringe. I assume it's grown
like Oscar Wilde's who imitated Emperor Nero.

    Camera Operator blushes:
Duplication is by de facto our unisonian.
Look even how conspicuously Ms Begum Jaan
wear pussy bow tie in honour of Miss Lottie
aka Ms Charlotte Mew & her poetry.

3

Mr Common Man's vision for Babu

On the setting of the venue, & Babu as the language
to reunite the Indo-European languages

〰

CHORUS:
Our troubadours, from the multitudinous nooks
(albeit they are seated around a table)
are viewed perambulating eyes about the room
because each poet can rarely dekko in full
their neighbouring rhymester for such is the rupture
of Bulbul Hall. Hall is the measure of a pub
for patron in flat cap but view again – what the,
what!? Hall seem to open its jaws & is magnol-
ious as Duuuurbar Hall but viewed again is pub
for handful patron in corner supping pale ale.
So bonkers a vista were never to be seen
if round the bend were to be seen, say, Taj Mahal.
Plus also, from each poet is heard a lone din
for they are rehearsing own lines aloud. Yet no
poet can hear them – as though the set of high-low,
nigh-far were such a trickster because only when
      each poet lean forward a smidgeon
      are they heard then by the audience.

      Mr Desani presents the first poet:
My dear Mr Common Man, stage-named after our cartoon,
with your broom moustache & Nehru collar standing firm

over your humble lungi, how will all cock-a-hoop
if they vacation, why, through our Brandenburg of Babu?

Mr Common Man, smiling, says:
I shall recite in the poulter's measure,
that common or garden fourteener.

Mr Common Man stands up to recite his poem

What words go old-boot lost in the desert like
                    tiger-cries
for rain sound? What handicraft way with sense
                    can untie
us from the mind blocks of 'in living memory'
                    & retrieve
the open mouths of merchants exchanging tales
                    in Attic
Sanskrit – 'twas our imagination's fons
                    et origo.
Let's go spry through a flower market with its stalls
                    stretching
for a porch-door that opes to a chatty forest.
                    Who'll sing
for that past? What færily haunts the heart's Bandusian
                    spring –
let's net it for indioms!? This mahal where all is
                    rinsed
de-luxe for new age. Lingo, sun-white as Neasden
                    mandir.
This sound potlatch, this Romantic dream, this breakage
                    filling
        Babu till it's our Proto-Indo-Euro
                    homecoming

that Max Muller saw holistic across the sky
       blissed with

Gold Ring.

*Applause upon wah-wahs fill Bulbul Hall, as they will each time a poem
is heard; there is no feedback for each poem in today's session*

4

The role of heritage for poets of colour

On the importance of keeping language alive, & how
poets of colour should be read

Mr Vishnoodas Desani stands up & faces the poets while he speaks

Mr Desani says:
We must honour the plenitude of language that's in verse.
What artifice if we're trapped in a modern aesthetic.
Let us hunt with our nets for even a limb of the worst
lawn, when we know that lawn has been displaced by
    synthetic
        squarehoods of earth-suffocating green.
        We salute you Mr Common Man.

Apachi Brummy, who'll recite later, says:
OMG, TBH I dig Max Muller, da dude state
we never hear da root of da word – only da upshot.
Words under surface are muscly as holy Oms!

Mr Vishnoodas Desani replies:
Indeed, youngster. Our dear Mr Empson once suggest words
that in our era are an umbrage, such as, say, fool, was
once an endearment. He termed such words, period flavours.

Mr Common Man, smiling, adds:
Was not Mr Empson bearded. It issue from under

his chin – down into neck. Back-to-front, his
dangling spaghetti, is not now a period flavour!

Camera Operator whispers to Director:
How should the viewer read each POC,
should Poets of Colour be read for content?

Director whispers:
Read weak POC for content, but quality POC –
read them for the way style can rocket heads clean off.

Camera Operator:
If a POC has curfewed a bullet behind the lips –
is very unthoroughly a recipe for riding a rocket!

Director:
All good POC-ery risks us down the ginnel
where we feel the nipples of a bittersweet kiss.

Camera Operator has light bulb moment:
I see, each POC is speaking its good grief
from beneath the tongue of the canon, & we,
the reader, must feel the jiggery POC-ery.

CHORUS:
Director & Camera Operator, smiling, say
to each other the mantra, *Know thy Blighty,
Know thy Blighty.* Then their palms are raised
for a high five aka talee.

Ms Begum Jaan & Coolie language

*On God's preferred language which might be Coolie,
how some Coolies trust a live performance, & can
'anger' be called 'bitterness'*

Mr Desani has been introducing the next poet:
. . . is why we'll now hoick our ears for Ms Begum Jaan.
She's our most reeking rebel blowing one too liberal
a smoke ring from her Krishna bidi, each ring's big & loose
as a line of unused nooses. Why, Ms Jaan you are con-
spicuous as Ms Charlotte Mew in a pussy bow tie.
Now if you would, let those rose lips puff their Coolie fettle
for your piece, I believe, in defence of Nissim, titled
'God Chunter in Coolie for Ordering Pizza in Heaven'.

Ms Begum Jaan smiles at Mr Desani:
Me no bond-servant! Me no, when yoo wanting, speak.

Mr Desani, unfazed, says:
Ms Begum Jaan, you remind us the art of the rebel
slave. We doff your refusal to script your work in the full
anglais. I hear you'll poeticise in the crude Russian,
the funny folksy chastushka song for your corruptions.

Ms Begum Jaan stubs her cigarette then recites

god chunter in Coolie for ordering pizza at heaven

coolie coolie hum hum
gully gully gum gum
me no badmaash lafunga
me no bandicoot dungar

!!!

ven Bhagwan rumble-tumble
gully gully for grumble
in dup dup heaven mall
he shout *coolie coolie angelll,*

!!!

cooking chicken tikka masala pizza
wid gharam gharam jaada
or my shakti-hutttt
feel ittt hot yor butt

Mr Desani focuses on an excited poet:
Though all collectorate has applauded,
one here is still stood – Ms Homi Bibi
who's hands-to-hand & hooting like hell,
discombobulus by this pell mell.

Ms Homi Bibi finally stops clapping & sits down

Camera Operator asks Director:
Why was Ms Begum Jaan, in Green Room, distrust
this lingo we indulge like a night in Tollygunge?

Director whispers:
You've been in absentia from Ind to recall
how her caste of toilet cleaners, manual
scavengers, find bolly is de facto oppressive.
They're peeved when our mahatmas prioritise
the written word over their rural orals –
she comes alive when treading the boards.

Camera Operator whispers:
Now I appreciate Ms Begum Jaan –
her antic of defiance. But how oft
they – the privileged – term this tone
of the great unwashed, via a mock-
humility or pride, as 'bitterness'.
They act incredulous that this underclass
waste the spotlight with this bold brass.

Director whispers:
Since #BLM our Indians who've their bread
buttered, with finest ghee, will not address
such matters as 'bitter'. Instead, 'frustrated'
may become the new way to cut them dead.

Camera Operator whispers:
Were we actors, thus seen & heard in *indiom* –
we may have directed talk to 'bitter' topic.

6

Inheriting Poets of Colour

On the influence of the original poets of colour who
wrote in English, & what political position Babu
poets might adopt

CHORUS:
Director's Assistant is behind Director but
is far enough that they seem below him, sat
looked up at his face. They're seen in a harmonium
which is gleaming & mounted on a podium.
Director watch their chortling with such relish
that he ask what is it? They spill their poetics.

*Director turns back & downwards to hear Director's Assistant speak about
the neglect of poets of colour in the early years of the internet*

I'll reveal old cause through the Masnavi form,
how we'd hide the red face within our own 'race'.

When the world first met on the internet
& our poets exchanged in a private space –

each felt only sought as performance poet.
We make our sadness known or stay on own?

In the fringe, we stayed tight. I dig up online
an archival thread in which our POC spread

solace through a poem they felt at home in.
In his thread, what I see – Apachi Brummy

like a cop with stealthy hand give Common Man
that text, whose black waters Common Man diffuse

to Begum Jaan, who blooter to Dai Pitta
the monkeying tone – her throat – she's feeling choked

till Gussama Beenon say, 'the inversion –
the self-mockery might elevate us free,

shame-free'. Saed Saed wonders, 'we're valley'd
poets for whom time will leapfrog from its bag

& we'll be a critical mass in the mass;
till then, let's lingo in peace sharing our grief'.

Some seek to become the Indic 'chosen one',
the next Nobel Tagore! The chat goes wound-sore.

One says, 'Tagore fought for reason, yet 'they' sought
his mystic mumbo – who'd next don those white robes!?'

All who played ceiling tennis to, at best, sit
in library or be pulped eternally,

those on whose shoulders we stand deserve honours,
it's our first canon – let's save it from Anon!

But what roused so much fuss was the past discussed
in its mutual stink by Wole Soyinka,

in '60s – his search for home in *Telephone
Conversation*. Reprieved by Homi Bibi

who once share her version with our POC online,
her take on the satire's best read as panegyre.

Homi Bibi is asked to read her version of a section of Wole Soyinka's poem

A man phone a landlady
re. a vacancy –
from straight-off, she's peeved,

'I've heard your voice & I'd seek
to inquire – tell me
you are a darkie?'

Still on phone Wole emote,
'Me face is brunette,
de soles of me feet,

dese palms, if you saw up close
are peroxide blondes
like dis big ole nose,

BUT dearie me, me lady
I been too lazy,
all day long I lay

about de big bad jungle
till one part go rum –
oh me black black bum!'

*Ms Begum Jaan, while off set, overhears this conversation about
Mr Soyinka's poem*

Director whispers to Camera Operator:
So down the 'rabbit' hole from Apachi Brummy
to Common Man, from Begum Jaan to Homi Bibi,
all have tapped into this 'call'. With each inheritor
become empire's creditor.

Camera Operator replies:
Wole's poem find home. If Nissim sought a mode
sounding authentic as an utterance – how can we
support Babu to bask in ubiquitous abode?

CHORUS:
Ms Begum Jaan smoking her Krishna bidi, hear the aside
& wonder – *Telephone Conversation* not in rabbit hole,
has become global studied poem. Plus, many have avail
through empire, such as Director's kin. Is it his right
to claim credit? Such as his kind ennobled empire
filling own boots while many of us aspired
for rice. To defend this Tomming is centrist stance,
should we poor let them claim the dirt of indigence?
She decides it's best to keep her own counsel.

Meanwhile, it seems Director has just spied
Camera Operator raise his left arm from inside
his lemon-yellow jean jacket to scruff his
hair which shifts its black a tad, like a wig.

7

Kutcha Butcha fears for the poets

On Kutcha Butcha's upbringing, & the implicit influence of Latin on English as his poem speaks of fear for the poet's safety

Cameras return to the table where the poets are seated

Mr Desani introduces the next poet:
Kutcha Butcha will recite next. Puppet for us your brewed
hauteur. Were you not like many here – an autodidact
who imbibed the glossaries yet who could never practise
his learning, who was never calibrated suitable
for the milieu of his adulthood, who'd become a bull
that must escape the maze of his hard-fast familial.

A camera catches Kutcha Butcha place his Tacitus,
which is in Latin, on the desk

Kutcha Butcha, says, before reciting his poem:
You've all apprised I ascend from gutter terrae filius
yet I presently scratch my collar for I am bilious
at the fear for us poets in a land where liberium
oratio is an oracle in peril. Here is my versum.

Kutcha Butcha recites his kavya, his poem, in a medium-high Babu

From my cathedra, where I sit obliquatum, in this
        Shardul Vikridit

metre, this tiger's play, where I propagate
    a convent smile to confess
these Janus contortions leave me devoured, no,
    I mean empowered.
I left on Thursday, when I don't wash my kesh,
    & now you let slip it's Tuesday;
does this Frank Gehri with its nips & tucks
    keep me from contextualisation?
This virtutis in action whereby non-history remain
    under false walls
like the servants, in a private bedlam, kept from our gaze
    or up or downwards
is there a hid land of fantastic grottoes, huts?
    Yet I feel in this terra
nihilus, we radicals might be under lock & key
    for the change we'll feel –
the travelling cross-hairs of a cybernetic –
    a drone head instructed to
            hit!

    Director whispers to Camera Operator:
Focus on our commander. He is youthless
being ringed with age, yet he's youthful
as appeared Satan in cherub dress
at Eden's gates where he doff a celestial
shanti. Our capitaan knows our talkie is satire
in a satire – thus no harm comes of 'the rise'.

    Mr Desani speaks to the collectorate:
Where the clocks do not tock well at this elevation,
we are off the plains nearer the imagined heavens.
Kutcha Butcha, I wish you find peace in a harbour
or hover freely forever – a lingo martyr.

CANTO I | [27]

8

Saed Saed's gay empire

On the empire's same-sex engagements which were
silenced, & Section 420 of the Indian penal code

◡

Director says to Camera Operator:
I must admit, you have a smile like semolina
hung out to dry on washing line in hawelli;
have you ever engaged in modicums of modelling –
no? It would be most befitting.

Camera Operator, inspired, replies:
I do not doubt you also would give excellent mileage
to a glossy cover. But look at our next poet's melange.
I see in *Namaste!* magazine – a headline, 'Our poet
these days are Cavalier!' I read how Saed Saed
attend a themed bash. Our scribblers were glad-rag
as 1630s poets – a fashion 'twas already old hat
in its inception. Saed Saed in a pic seen guzzle
mead & wear Turkish doublet, plus Parisian breeches
with tapered fringes – yes, lace dangling from his knees.

Director is amused & strokes his hair which moves a little, as a wig might

Director says to Camera Operator:
Saed Saed's excavation of the literary past is apt
when the globe has been pawed & stomped,
& no exotic zone remains. Let each man jack

cutlass the national forest of their literary hinterland
to alight upon the neglected asphodels of their swamp.
 Know thy Blighty.

 Camera Operator, clasping his hands, agrees:
Know thy Blighty.

 Saed Saed introduces his poem:
As a Cavalier poet of yore, I wish to revive the yore
& when I recite my poem in a soft fruity score
of time's trans-shifting & forgotten subversions,
let soft fruity music underscore my rendition
for every at-it empire general, sahib, sircar, milord.
 I'll recite my poem in the piplikamadhya,
 a metre which gives my zhuzh a hutzpah.

Exotic music serves as background while Saed Saed recites his poem

Was empire ruled by men forlorn of own women
 for amour, stuck in excess of
TEMPERANCE to help their missionary 'burden'?

Hot for harem? No, instead sahib is prancey
 for rear game at tiffin! He's shucked
in Great Hedge with Coolie & Babu doxy –

his mock-Roman charver, his bush-bash hidden
 tale! There was one cut-throat blessing,
fewer village filly raped (who give birth to strewn

kiddiwink (kick the bastard from village – is cursed)).
 Queer love is clean love! Sugar & spice,
& all things polyglot across the continents.

Raj like 'scorched earth policy', the Crown's hour may fade.
　　　Oh come, man-hunting memsahib
virgins! Jaldi please, from the shires to bag – nay, save

tupping Tommies! *Eastward ho!* P&O liner
　　　beefed with toff donas who plead con-
science to each fallen sahib. Then jumping over

broomstick with her gent, married, she stiff his tongue
　　　pristine – but once he have subord-
inate his libertine rose, his sobbing budbud.

*Saed Saed sits down & music recedes, Mr Desani cracks a walnut
with two fingers*

　　　Mr Desani says:
History has endless folds in time. How do we open
just a fold so it expose a truth – raw as a stonking
lesion. A truth that will not beget fear & flag-waving
that leads to an army rushed in-fear to save its nation.

Camera is close-up on Saed Saed's blue eyes (owing to his contact lens)

　　　Saed Saed returns to his own concern:
India's anti-thuggery act today – Section 377,
was shafted-in by the Raj. Is modelled on
Henry VIII's buggery act. All time is one.
　　　We are in a midst of a midst –
　　　all Blighty in a midnight tryst.

　　　Mr Desani replies:
Code 377 reminds me that char-soh-vee, our
420 penal code can condemn any who fall foul –
who foul fall in any way! So this law of deception
means all who are born in Ind are, de facto, born in sin!

        Saed Saed, smiling, replies:
But we're not scuppered in ganga-jammed
History. It treads with us like rouge carpet
under foot. At times, carpet is rummed
with blood peeping through the fabric,
other times & places – carpet is crimson
as a Cavalier who's decked for pageant!

        CHORUS:
It's known hill stations are inhabited by ghouls,
some images now flicker on the walls of Bulbul Hall.
The hills are seen brimmed with ghosts of empire.
A cart of satsumas turns into skulls, a golden-hair
but dead woman is heard shrieking at the vision
of her lover whose face is illuminated in heaven.
The ghost of a British doctor from the Raj spooks
a living Indic surgeon, at work, who's near snoozing.

9

Ms Gussama Beenon on forgiveness

On how not all poets of colour can be read from a
leftie perspective, & the healing powers of Babu

Mr Desani introduces the next poet:
Now I'll summon a poet born back when, in the ole days
when Babu's served to the endgame administering Part
-ition. One with an encyclopaedic vim, yet she lays
a modest lay for she speaks of all folk, in her heartfelt
indioms. Ms Gussama Beenon, of your poetic
oeuvre – should we analyse it wielding the angry axe
of Marxism? For us brown poets, yes – this seems legit.
Yet I fear it is a blunt bandana critique – a lax
reduction if Ms Beenon prove a traditionalist.
Ms Gussama Beenon, who bear the stripes of the ten
guru nation of Punjab – bear us your pigmentation
(on a migrant appetite for bankroll that's never waxed).

Director whispers to Camera Operator:
Zoom-in now with all cameras amply succulent
for Ms Gussama Kaur Beenon who have neck elegant
as a bottle of milk stout. Her wrinkled knuckles
& that face stately aged grand as Ms Grace Nichols.

Camera Operator replies:
Our cinematographer, she's a colour-pride technician,
she's set lighting on perfect percentage of reflectance,

each brown skin is nuanced with subtle shades
as Spike Lee talkies entitle our grief its grace.

   Ms Gussama Beenon addresses poets:
Mr Vishnoodas, my dear troubadours, I've brought
with me a kavya which aids my nexus
through the complex woods of inbetweenness.
I am all for the gravitas of the heart's core
& hope my lines create a huggable rapport.

Ms Beenon recites her poem composed in medium Babu

My Punjabs say I went off white,
        my English friends they mock my accent;
two rutputty homes I shored
        against my moht with a lingua hoard.

My breath, how shall I say, say, 'wind'?
        Call it wind or havaa? One is
the breath-nipped shunt, but my other,
        which is the baaj today for this

anecdote, told in anushtubh
        metre, as it were, is havaa,
its 'v' like a kiss smiling up
        on lips to blow like a lover.

Havaa, havaa. I say, havaa
        is what I feel from our alpine
saah for my home, my class.
        Can I, by ad-interim mean

such as this sift, sift to find words
        freed from the hurt of kidhood jarred

in my noggin like roman roads,
        so my havaa's built to be haar?

        Camera Operator whispers to Director:
Lovely it is, our Cavalier, Saed Saed is laying a haar,
a garland, over Ms Beenon's neck. Is on my mike
heard – is the cruffly static sound, is on contact with her
cardigan. Ah the live wires of market fabric!

        Saed Saed states for all poets to hear:
Those scotty Scots, you know Hugh MacDiarmid
or James Kelman, they blether for the tribal sound fit
for their oorlich we-ness weather. Let's not be scotched
from forking our fringe voice – it's a migrant prerogative.

        Ms Gussama Beenon adds:
As every fringe is a frontier, let the bolly we've builded
be centred in its own greenbelt. Dal dy dir for gadding.

10

Apachi Brummy & Indian youth

On the youth of India being unduly influenced by
America, & Mr Desani's disapproval of a negative
tone

      Director says to Camera Operator:
Who's not enamoured by the livewires of market fabric?
I tell you who, our next troubadour. They can do without,
they are too cool by half. I speak of a spoken word patriot/
        standup comedian/swallower of sword/
        Apachi Brummy who adopt accent
        & Jafaican of Kate Tempest
        when giving full vent
        (a digress, in few weeks Kate
        will identify as Kae).

Apachi Brummy waves his arms passionately in preparation
for his syllables, then recites his poem

Why's Yankee cola-talk vogue?
Dem States mickey-take dis tongue.

Deirs is a coolie slang chat!
      Even our hoity Brahmin
bro thique outa' deir private
      tuition on da lane spit

paan thru dese fixed syllables
    with a motherfuckerin'
& a *yo!* & a *dang!* All
    our Bharat droogs are swingin'

on back issues of *Fuck You*,
    'what's sick in Covent Garden,
we'll match deir Greenwich cool'.
    Dey'll eat our Bhuna mutton

& Madras BUT refusenik
our gastro gutsy Babu.

    Mr Desani, surprised by the tone, replies:
Be a grinch Mr Apachi? We are pleased this dithy-
ramb was in syllabics, but Babu is utopian,
is pantisocratic – loving all creative action.
Dear rapscallion, look outside. Each daffadowndilly
in stupendous ascension. Though some after slumber will
seldom rise like *Lion King* lions in gilt livery
or pimp a butterfly – being not daffodilian
brandished. Or, being poor in their powers, cannot avail
us with beauty, say, as a radish can aid digestion.
However bleak or staunch each daffadowndilly, yet all
    in their birth contract give off the oils
    umbilical to our youngblood soil.

    Camera Operator whispers to Director:
Is there tension here – tension could doofus to tongue-slap?
But Babu is hospitality. We are like those elaborate sal-
laams of yore, the brief 'salut' on the bridge to salvation.

    Director replies not looking at Camera Operator:
As you talked, Apachi embraced magnanimous meekness.
He picked himself off the Floor of Regret to finesse

himself up on metaphorical stilts. From those stilts
      Apache is now hugging from on-facetious
           high with Mr Vishnoodas.
      Let's admire their elongated legs of gravitas.

      Camera Operator replies:
On lawn outside – the flash in a shell of a tucked-in
tortoise by Mr Vishnoodas Desani's diamond ring
is caught by our cameras who implanted, inside
a tortoise, micro-camera, while it was lain on lawn.

11

Tiffin!

On the serving of tiffin, & how poets should enjoy
themselves so their wit can be maximised

CHORUS:

Mr Vishnoodas is now seen walk-
ing, as if on a wall,
each space between tables seem lane-
like; while walking, in & out, down
straight ahead yet elevating maze-
or up the path, he call:
Parishioners, thirsty for potables? For a sup
named after an Indian number, punj,
five, for its ingredient totality, Punch?

Everyone raise five backward fingers
lighting the screen with nail varnish,
bangle, bracelet & gold ring
while cracking complimentary laughter.
>   Punch is served
>   as deserved!

Poets are seen chatting & drinking

>   Mr Desani asserts:
Recall Francis Beaumont in his lay to Ben Jonson. He said,
in line 13, 'I think with one draught man's invention fades'.
& many draughts fired invention at the Mermaid Tavern,
let's be Jonson wit-combatting with the Swan of Avon,
let's be Mermaid troubadours onward from the Renaissance
>   or how else do we gad in the to-whit
>   forest of a national culture's wit?
>   No wit & the forest is brick built.

CHORUS:
Collectorate are seen everywhere hugging
across lower-appearing floor with those over
their heads. Choast, chalaak, droll, smart seeming
as Keats' when he supped canary wine. Ah Angostura!

Also, platters of eatables made by the best-caste
chef are presently dished. The womp of mogo chips laid
aside Ding Dong beef crispies – laid aside 1cwt
spread of drooped salad which each hand must appreciate
across for the tanginess of tan sustenance that
is heaped by each upon their spode plate.

Many are fast on the G-T road, at full speed,
while also gulping a garlic clove for the blood.
Many, while chatting, play cards, play swift
rounds of traditional games – ombre/basset.

CANTO

II

CANTO II

12

Profit for 'marginal' poets

On how to step out of the shadows of Standard
English, & on how the poets can win sympathy in
the West with a hardship narrative

Poets are still eating & drinking

Camera Operator whispers to Director:
Each camera have topknot of flashing red light,
cameras seem OFF. Poets speak their minds
not having twigged cameras are actually ON!
By perdition, I say, let's keep rolling incognito.
A wink, at me Mr Director? Yes, I am glad
you buy-in. We are very very sassy!

Ms Kuku Paku asks her fellow poets:
I hear Mr Desani refer to our jamboree as 'tragic
joy', in Green Room. How have we lose the magic?

Ms Homi Bibi replies:
Hai! Standard English – it's in our Hall!?
Does it host Babu like a poot-ghoul?

Mrs Dai Pitta is also inquisitive:
What hotty-botty! Mr Vishnoodas, ek-dum
stand up from these handstand press-ups,
answer us, please. Does Standard English call
us victims, or does it chat with us as equal?

Mr Vishnoodas takes a puff of air:
Your question should be, who invited it?
Answer – English is President of Precedent.

Ms Kaku Paku uses an 'old skool' slang:
Brown-skin melanin blues? Or we fear being surveyed
by the very lingo we 'dig' to exceed?
Does not the crow gawp at the peacock
as the scarecrow balks at the windsock.

Apache Brummy assumes cameras are off:
Ho! We'll not even draw flies – we gotta go high-low
to schmooze viewers on seats, from, you know,
dem Standard English aficionados?

Mr Vishnoodas sounds bitter:
British are classy, they'll put own money to the mouth;
as for our lot, put bums on seat? They'd never shell out.

Ms Japprey gives her peers an analogy:
Lest we forget, a poet nowadays neglected.
You know Ann Yearsley, the milkmaid poet,
she earned pittance per year, but her debut in 1785,
due to Albion's compassion for the marginalised,
crisped her with £500 fortune. If we can sell out
our poetry-as-news, we'll win us Yearsley's repute!

Gussama Beenon:
I heard Mr Desani say earlier – we've a migrant
appetite for making wealth that may never repent.

Apachi Brummy considers:
Ho! But we're, are we not – a luvvy set,
every dude a privilege VVIP bhadralok!

So in West, let's be as model minority – let's
be Coolies who lay da lines to socket da rocks!

Mr Nahasapeem have a polished manner:
Many Anglo-artist claim they're the four Yorkshiremen,
working class mythmakers of the Monty Python sketch.
They all furnish a hardship tale from where they descend,
let's copy the class poppycock of that 'self-made' set.

Mr Vishnoodas says:
Let us pave a mightier road. You know Mr Blackie's
A Song of Heroes – in its many lines, he was bereaved
by his peers. They 'sold Scotland's grace & honour for bags of
English gold'. Let's carpe diem, with no heed for profit,
rose beds of indioms! Aught else is fool's gold, poppycock.

CHORUS:
All poets clasp their hands & repeat, after
Mr Desani, their famed mantra.
        Know
            thy Blig hty   Kn
            o
            w   th   th
            y   y   Bl

        Bl   b   l
            i
                    ght   Knnn   w

    yyyyyy   Blii   ghh ty   Kn light.

13

Ms Homi Bibi's Coolie dream

On the virtues of Coolie-English, & how Babu is
part of a counter voice that runs alongside Standard
English

〰

*Poets now assume the cameras are all turned on & expect
a formal invitation for the next poet to speak*

Ms Homi Bibi stands abruptly & calls out:
Well here's a young shokri – I'm Homi Bibi
I'm a katzenjammer who's goofed as a bear
with laughalong smiley. Oh what do I care
if my words be 'Hungry' or 'Naked' akavis!

Ms Homi Bibi is dancing as she recites her akavi in a high Coolie

newness is whatwhat heard   baaj
gutter butter buk   buk   gurbur
jeeb jalebi   bolly   bhaji   kaaj
utter   mutter butter gutter gulsh
bolly   kaaj   dil-vil   baaj butter
jeeb   jalebi   geegaw   bolly
geet   kaaj   bolly   baat   gurbur
gutter   butter buk   buk   kaaj
gutter   butter buk   buk   baaj
dil-vil-dil-vil-dil-vil-dil-vil-dil-oyvey

Mr Vishnoodas Desani, laughing, says:
What furore poeticus, Ms Bibi. I endear
your Siva arms in a kathak, in a kathak dance.
Why stand the gas of that Horation middle distance!
Permit me to term your song Baboolie. Such Eeyore
of incorrigible plurality's been in the dark
alongside Mr Milton's Populo Anglicano.
Eeyore individualism has been repressed for 4-
00 years, yet Orwellian plainspeak's a de rigueur.

Ms Homi Bibi replies to Mr Desani:
Hai gin-gurgling, mela-man! De-rigeurism
is Excel buk-buk, is buk-buk by algorithm,
is buk-buk for matriculation,
is rigor mortis for imagination!

Camera Operator whispers to Director:
At outset of recital, Ms Homi Bibi
had fuddled temples – yet her skin, with every
Baboolie line become incrementally creamy.

Director faces camera to say:
Speaking English is enlightening.

> Apache Brummy walks over to the Director
> & raises his top to bare his chest

Apachi Brummy whispers to Director:
Ho! droog, my chest too is goin' gora! I feel it prosper
fresh at dawn, roarin' out da hammock, when I strut
da boards emulatin' Sir Gielgud as Hotspur.

14

Montage of British-Indians

*On some successful Indians in Britain, & the politics
of the Indian head loll*

🪶

CHORUS:
Camera crew go on walkies to place cameras upon
images in the multiple-seeming floors of Bulbul Hall.
They show a painting by Singh Twins – its brawl
(in watercolour titled 'EnTWINed') has Henry Nelson
O'Neil's image of the mutiny *Eastward Ho!*
slapped over with images of nowadays uber-cool
demi-Indos in the Cool Britannyo!

A *you-want-some-douchebag!* housewife who grasp
steak knife – she's Kali, in acrylic by Supta Biswas,
with men heads hung on her necklace.

Such art, it's hard to decide whether it's aloft
in foreground or in rear of the capacious hall.
Is such positioning itself a simile for token
or merited elevation of Indics in Britain!?
Answer's black & white: if only one alone
is summoned from our sum for a commission –
                    one is token!

Cameras next show image of a blue plaque
(in 2020's erected in Bloomsbury) for our wahwah
spy of Sufi, Noor Khan. Arrested, cracked

by bullet at Dachau – Noor's cry from the heart
was not well known Bollywood *bachao!!!*
As befit every abducted maiden – was *liberté*.

How Babu to be Français! How Babu to say ciao
with peach cheeks like Delacroix's lady of *Liberté*.

Seb Coe is shown, fastest ever Punjab, who 'pass'
like Freddie Mercury, our mustachio Parsi.

     Director whispers to Camera Operator:
Some may 'pass' to never champion Ind –
never ballyhooing us as being cool. What's
unlikely appreciated by our audience, is our head loll.

The Indian head loll have a complex lexicon. Install
for me a dumb show of *your* head; bereft it of thought
then let it sidle idly side to side – lolling on the spot.

     Camera Operator, pats his pencil eyebrows:
I'm lolling – is hard with no connectivity of intellect
to maintain a fulsome loll-rolled. Is giving my neck
a mauling! Is like having a rickle of tomes career
on your head while reading *Riverside Shakespeare*.

     Director replies:
There is a head loll for 'mauling' which is specifically
achieved if one lolls from first to fourth gear abruptly.

> *While Camera Operator practises this head loll, Director is seen*
> *stroking the Camera Operator's neck without actually touching*
> *the neck, in a way that is similar to reiki*

     Director replies to Camera Operator:
Who is not 'true Indian', not descended from the cut–

thrust of Ind could never acclimatise to all this head chat stretching from Blighty to Bharat. Babu's emboldened, enriched by this bidirectional banter of a head stroll.

15

Mr Nahasapeem & Ms Nasneen on *The Simpsons*

On the significance of Indians who live in Britain, &
their treatment through humour

CHORUS:
On screens, across the room is now been shown
montage from *The Simpsons* of Apu posed
behind Kwik-E-Mart counter, he's swearing
with the many arms of Vishnu about whatever it is,
though he's flapping we can't hold laughing.

Montage of The Simpsons *stops, Mr Nahasapeem & Ms Nasneen speak
about Indians in Britain after World War II*

Mr Nahasapeem, in the regale metre:
This huff-snuff Apu's a stereotype,
thus not a lifestyle worthy of its scribe.

CHORUS:
A high-Coolie is come from Ms Nasneen
who emulate her neighbour with regale metre,
Ms Nasneen's like Mindy of *The Mindy Project*
after whom she broke from the lexis-wall man built
(noting chumcha is spoon but said as self-insult).

Ms Nasneen says to Mr Nahasapeem:
They work five days, we is chumcha 24/7,
we build Britain – Empire shop feel it is no shutdown.

Mr Nahasapeem replies in kind:
Ergo madam, there's no time for breeding
like rabbits – why, we are nation breeding.
We've made our host mighty, he must be meek or mock
& retrieve some pride, which is why we're gagged for joke.

Ms Nasneen replies in kind:
Is true Mr Nahasapeem, when on idiot box
our actor is shoogly, is always shop-wallah, doctor.

CHORUS:
Mr Nahasapeem, whose past have some disaster,
self-made now for his own Indic novelty shop
in Southall, where Ms Nasneen have job.
He's so civil to show who is the master!

Mr Nahasapeem replies to Ms Nasneen:
Those Simpsons, they make a serial attack,
their regular team with its guest writers make
like white men laughing while in the queue
to be in the head of our Apu.

Ms Nasneen replies on a cheerier note:
This Apu make India sound it love all caste,
I love this Apu, I love you have Babu past;
you make me laugh – you singing Bollywood song
in storeroom, my chai cup is four sugar strong!

Mr Nahasapeem replies cheerfully:
Shopkeepers should homage their shelves
with fresh Lamborghinis
of grammar, with pulled rickshaws of hawker
hootenannys!

Ms Nasneen continues the nonsense:
All shopkeeping – please please jaggery the wedding
bedding, so couple they start new life with giggling.

Director whispers to Camera Operator:
Oft in a poetry rally this is the cognisance –
what's under wraps-at-work's free as a prince.
Ms Nasneen is moving close to Mr Nahasapeem.
What carpe diem! What midsummer night's dream!

Camera Operator says he will attempt replying in non-Babu

Camera Operator says to Director:
We love to know & share our knowing with those
who love to know we know just as they know,
from such knowing true love gateau the meadow.

Director makes soft applause:
You nearly have it, excepting 'gateau the meadow'.
Standard English easy spills from one's wheelbarrow.

Camera Operator replies:
Charles Olson call the pentameter & its slick palate
'a honey head'. Too sweet – it stogged his testy gut.

Director replies:
Mr Nahasapeem is savouring Ms Nasneen's smile,
he had no feel for her being such a Chicken 65.

Mr Nahasapeem says to Ms Nasneen:
Whose hooting, when in *Bird Box* Ms Nagra's an Indian,
& doctor. She alone in talkie wore a fake accent.

Ms Nasneen, near completing him:
Why she not boll in own voice – is she from Midland?

Mr Nahasapeem completing her:
Ergo, her Leicester accent, that hotchpotch, more so
than Indian must cause greater LOL guffaw.

Director feels rushed:
Camera Operator – oh fast
she's moving over to – he's gasped
by her – are they? They pucker for a
smooch. I'm raising a How's-Your-Father
alert, now! We're not a five
rupee bodice-ripping – I shiv-
er my timbre – Coolie & Babu kiss.

Camera Operator replies:
We mustn't be a basium genre,
lo! those choomy, kiss, text writ by
Secundus, a lingo that's peculiar
as Nissim's Miss Puspha T.S. lines,

   'one kiss, mesmeric maid, I cried,
   one petty kiss, then au revoir
   to lips with fruity crimson dyed'.

16

Director & Populous Shutup

On a Populous Shutup across the world & its impli-
cations for writers & for humans in general

CHORUS:
Director does not reply but he's cognisant
basium mode of choomy cause disgustment
presently on snog-banned, choomy for chumps, planet.
Snog-ban? Betroubled planet? In Spring 2020, what!?

Director overhear Apache Brummy, who knit
a mandala weave with Miss Homi Bibi;
yes, they are knitting a multicoloured hanging
which will be for Bulbul Hall their parting gift.
Anyroad, Apache say that he has a gripe,
though they're a super group that can recite
poems for non-stop weeks – weeks *are* passing!
So why are they still at it, albeit they're hot-trot
happy? Director will explain. He is rush off,
rushing-up for Hoover cupboard, which is stored
with no end of lavatorial paper. He's followed,
& hear tripping over in this pigsty, over
an iron for ironing crease into 501s, Camera Op-
erator.

Director whispers to Camera Operator:
I speak in Alexandrines to hit the kernel
which none have discerned – that we're sailing into false

colours, let's say. The shower-arrows of April
have been soot! Yet we're feeling fired-up having stayed
safe in domus, yet we must stay weeks stoked indoors!
There is a Populous Shutup! Shutup! Yes, I swear
everyone is stuck indoors. This Shutup's same-same
on planet! Amitav Ghosh, author, once declare
Great Derangement's our Ship of Death – if writers fail
to forecast the gloom & win us from a Shutup.
It mean our whole building been straightjacketed. Nil
by leaving out has been a single ant. Nil by
leaving in has been a beetle. We are bound as
an intrepid silken ribbon round a giftbox
except we have black-yellow cordon that has tied
us, all over – it's wrapped unfathomable as
a QR code. Who knows the way of yellow tape –
it grasp even a lightbulb that has, b'gum, lost
its cover. Oh Victorian streetlamp, that has
by one gloop of glue-tape stayed gooed on the live bulb.
What else – we *all* must be shielded in the Shutup
because of our subterranean condition,
our dire undercurrent condition, Indian.

Camera Operator holds an iron & its unspooled flex in the storeroom

Camera Operator says to Director:
We glory god with a lip-licking dine
of every brinded-beauty bestially pied.

Director, near broom-bristles, replies:
For our pieding & shystering we've Shutup us aboard
a nunnery deck of Babu Hopkins' *Deutschland*.

Camera Operator, nervously, says:
The antidote to the upshot of our bold
helm will be a shot in the arm for lingo.
New words will be flavour for a period.

Darkness à la mode Mr Shandy

On a card held before the talkie screen

BLANK SCREEN darken the entire set
for a silent, for a noir, kala, nada minute.
BLANK SCREEN darken the entire set
for a silent, for a noir, kala, nada minute.
BLANK SCREEN darken the entire set
for a silent, for a noir, kala, nada minute.
BLANK SCREEN darken the entire set
for a silent, for a noir, kala, nada minute.
BLANK SCREEN darken the entire set
for a silent, for a noir, kala, nada minute
à la mode Mr Tristram Shandy when a page block
itself in black to pine alas for death of Mr Yorick.

Playing Hobson-Jobson & Hanklyn-Janklin

On a word game where two glossaries, inspired by
the Raj, are used, & how good humour is maintained

Camera Operator whispers to Director:
Now what is happen, clapping is rise
being nursed to cheers, but why?
You have tell of Populous Shutup
to Mr Vishnoodas? Yes. So instead
of hearing next poet or world in mess,
in a six pence, they've change tack
inspired by Mr Stoppard's *India Ink*,
hijinks game should keep our poets
distracted from elongated session
till is arriving Intermission.

Director replies:
They'll write poems with as many words as possible
from Hanklyn-Janklin & Hobson-Jobson,
these glossaries house words that were most
commonly used by our masters, these manifold
words & phrases come from 100-plus Indic lingos.

Camera Operator replies:
Yes, I agree, let's be gone walks-talking 'on a wall'
so we freely talk.

Director:
These glossaries are like English Roast as a mishmash
of roasted souffle with sides of churros & denim lasagne.

Camera Operator, laughing:
Truly, I hear the sound itself of Hobson-Jobson
is from the Muslim, 'Ya Hasan! Ya Hosain!',
the musalman chant 'Ya Hasan! Ya Hosain!'
the empire hear 'Hobson-Jobson'.
Is how diction chukk new sock on.

Poets are seen composing their poems

Director chukk, raise, a fresh insight:
Several troubadours peek a gilded antiquarian.
Mostly Mr Virgil from their back or bra pocket;
but please assume – in Indian talkie of this text
poet in pockets will be an Indic Dionysian!

Camera Operator holds up three postcards:
But of my posterior pocket, you've not been entice
to see what peeks early doors? I've three postcards
& each is a sketch said to be made by the Francophile
Mr Beckett. Each pencil sketch is of a smile that regards
the face of Mr Alighieri as he is guided through lower-
mid-&-ooper world by Mr Virgil in his *Divina
Commedia*. Each day, I raise like mirror a carded smile
that best suits my smile for the up-low of my daily trial.

Director quizzes Camera Operator:
But what humour you regard as this talkie's aim?
Are we inbetweeners rendered plastic as cartoons?
Or do we laugh profoundly at two sides who claim
a view so bigoted that they are driving grooves

for fences stuck into the backs of the public –
each divided being is always hearing a cricket
captain shouting to his fielding team, 'Boundrry,
boundrry, arrey bastards watch da boundrry!'
Let's conjecture this while poets play up,
play up, play up their vita lampada muckabout.

19

Camera crew on humour

On the preferred types of humour for overcoming
distress of a social & philosophical order

✺

Camera Crew make insights while filming the poets who play their word game

CHORUS:
Camera Crew interject to opine about laughter.
Is hard to say which crew member parleying after
the next; they're indiscernible & into their cameras necked.
What is seen, committee in game
composing Hobson/Janklin poem.
What is heard, some camera crew share views on humour,
(noting please, 'I' in Indic is 'hum').

Voices of Camera Crew are heard

hum hum likey a jackanapes subaltern riposte

hum hum likey laughter catching vice of 'leviathan' Hobbes

hum hum likey a Freudster laugh letting out pent-upness

hum doing laughter to unboycott my catarrh

hum for undicking the dickery by Cixous's Medusa

hum hum likey *The Beaches of Agnès* of Agnès Varda

where a body opened leads to a landscape –
open me I say & promenade
athwart me dunes of dunnock laughter

hum philosophise repetition as principle of existence
when our heads are baking hot with canon-cognisance
& unsure where to place like apple-pie its piping episteme

is why leela is making our smile so extreme
making it daft as a brush, all day,
the way Nissim compose his Pushpa lay

so what, hum still for undicking dickery by Cixous's Medusa!

  Director whispers to Camera Operator:
Keep it rolling – your camera crew is a league of grinners
like ghee wouldn't melt. Are Samuel Smiles & Pollyanna
cheering them onward? I feel as though each coolie crew
dude is recalling the custard pies of micro-aggro viewed
upon their shame-face BUT they fight back the custard
with bust-a-jouissance-&-breathless gut.

  Camera Operator replies:
So, the sum total for soaking up decades of being buffoon,
  of always smiling back, of sucking it
up, mean that each of these grins compound the kismet
  for a joie-de-vivre boon!!!

  Director replies:
I am enjoying your positivity. The cameras inhabit
Karl Popper's dictum, that only in talkie 'future coexist
  with past, so past to future's fixed'.
   In toto, if revered – time can be kind.

Camera Operator:
Look, the screen – Jacques Derrida is behind his desk,
he's in the talkie *Ghost Dance* & playing himself.
He's telling the camera that he must presently be seen
as a ghost of himself, because he's on the screen
& improvising for *Dance* talkie! Derrida show
we are hopping ghosts on the beaches with own ghost.

Director:
But who is the ghost? Nowadays even the Coolie,
once silent as the dead, is berating from his Pimlico
desk a man of Babu stock who's now his employee;
Babu tongue cowers behind the bosses snow globe!

Camera Operator:
Who is ghosting who is hard to capisce or QED.

20

Confessions of Director & Camera Operator

On a growing friendship, & who is truly the other in
a relationship

Camera team heard in the background as they chat & laugh

Director says to Camera Operator:
Inchoate excess laughter careers
to the autobahn of diarrhoea.

Camera Operator is understated:
No one is driving for WC.

Director glances at Camera Operator:
Btw, I'm loving your firm moustache
reminiscent of Mr Walcott's stash.

*Camera Operator keeps his manner understated as David Niven
(in one of his classic talkies)*

Camera Operator whispers to Director:
Your handlebar's equably a dashing
yet even-steven brush.

CHORUS:
Pair go colour of George Eliot's
handwriting – is aubergine.
Camera crew being so cheeky

insert odd scented wedding bells
that waft ambrosia & pilchards –
as the bells dong they evoke
a gross feeling of Roman candles
sighing hotly their O! O! O!
when each flame feels like a thousand
coily hairs enjoying being dithered.

Director looks ahead at the set as wedding bells cease their ringing

Director whispers to Camera Operator:
Look, you are stonkingly dark complexion, for sure,
but I'm not Mr Pound worrying that Ms Moore
might be dark & wooled (that's before he'd met her).

Camera Operator continues looking ahead at his Camera Crew

Camera Operator:
Did Mr Pound not say, 'could I have bridged the gap
to Ethiopia'. I'm glad the bridge was gap-free
when you walked it – oh my stonkingly dear man.

Director speaks softly as a drowsy perfume:
Even if you are bridged black as Mrs Blyton's Mafumu.

Camera Operator whispers his affection:
Even if you were darker than Dark Lady of Clerkenwell,
Lucy N-word, for whom our bard fell over head.

Director:
The unzipped & warm breeze across the facets
of Bulbul Hall is exceptional – the dusky brown
air these months has absconded! This attests
to the cleansing by Populous Shutup. Dear man,
I wish to cleanse some air, to make a clean breast.

It is decent to conclude, I am not who you assume
I'm. I am a lady. A lady attired as Director dude.

Camera Operator maintains a calm look:
How else to gainfully win us a lanyard for this activity,
            dear chap.
Knowing too, I am – I'm also not autobiographically
            a man.

Camera Operator turns to his back pocket

Camera Operator replies:
I've raised from my posterior – Mr Beckett sketch to extol
a smile that Mr Dante make when he's in paradiso.

Camera Operator smiles at the sketch; Director dances a little jig

Director makes an anatomical confession:
I've felt cursed by my Mr Byronic right foot,
this club stump. I never respected quite
the Lord as a poet with a bohemian limb.
This footloose *indiom* – my footwork is at home!

Camera Operator jokingly wonders if the Director has an itchy foot

Camera Operator:
Is your libido a light-foot like Mary Hamilton of Taunton?
Henry Fielding's 'hero', yes – they wed a baker's dozen
of ladies at least while impostered as George Hamilton.

Director, excited, replies:
I have a passage from that story, *The Female Husband*,
memoried to heart – when she was Dr George Hamilton
with Mary Price, a molly, a hot queer, & 18:

'. . . the two loverſ had an occaſion of dancing all night together; & the Doctor loſt no opportunity of ſhewing his fondneſſ, aſ, well by hiſ tongue aſ by hiſ handſ, whiſpering many ſoft thingſ in her earſ, & ſqueezing aſ many ſoft thingſ into her handſ, which, together with a good number of kiſſeſ, &c, ſo pleaſed & warmed thiſ poor girl, who never before had felt any of thoſe tender ſenſationſ which we call love, that ſhe retired from the dancing in a flutter of ſpiritſ, which her youth & ignorance could not well account for; but which did not ſuffer her to cloſe her eyeſ, either that morning or the next night.'

Both men are seen giving a hip shuffle as they echo each other

'Know thy Blighty'   'Know thy Blighty'

'Wife of Bath'   'Wife of Bath'

*Both men talee & laugh; resisting a little jig,
they continue 'walks-talking' about Bulbul Hall*

21

Duo Dharker's interview Nissim Ezekiel

On an interview with Nissim Ezekiel, in the 1990s,
about the poems he wrote in Babu English

*Ms Nasneen overheard the chat between Director
& Camera Operator that took place in shot 20*

Ms Nasneen whispers:
Is Screenwriter nose running to be full for sneezing?

Mr Nahasapeem, gleaming, replies:
Madam, you mean, she can't blow off tick-boxing allusions
to English. What if Babu's subversion by reverence?
Or we're so amour with English, yet fear its admittance?

Ms Nasneen replies:
If we bad on Blighty, is we failing Marmite test?
Not use own brain-dreaming, but be seen being wide-read.

Mr Vishnoodas Desani quietens the poets

Mr Desani says to everyone:
All here have the speed of clappers when chatting for
   England!
Hear this. Mr Nissim Ezekiel gave confession
when interviewed once by a whippersnapper couple. Fate
hath lost the transcript but I will now recollect the tale.

Nissim spoke of his kavya, poems, their use of humour,
when decades past he felt homeliness in an interview
with that brace, that intrepid journo & poet duo

Dharker 1 + Dharker 2 = ing Duo Dharkers!

Duo Dharkers distrust the whitewash of uva, are like
Eliot's 'bats with baby faces in the violet light';
they drive to Nissim's pad, their minds as ever Volvo-lit.

They circle his wagon, suppling questions – what a duo!
One is, why his laugh kavyas are the loved ones? His riposte,
gulping a glass of nimboo panee, 'When I give full clout

to my accent kavyas, yes, these were the ones the crowds
    loved,
but my peers scoff them. I wrote my verse based on what I
    heard,
is that wrong? Is that arrogance – is that empire hauteur?'

Duo Dharkers keep the recorder ON, Nissim is thankful
to share, 'These kavyas were a risk. I hope my *Coll-
ected Poems*, will surv—, you know, when I've popped my
    clogs.'

Popped or pawned just then, dear poets, Nissim is far from
    swell!
To uplift our bard, Duo Dharkers stand, sing a Hebrew Mel-
ody, 'She Walks in Beauty like the Night'. Just then, who fell

alongside Duo Dharkers to sing through his feeling of hearse,
standing & giving belly, plus hoping the best for his
Miss Pushpa goodbye poem, was, you know it yaar, Nissim!

Saed Saed, the Cavalier, asks Mr Desani:
Who are these velvet-caped newshounds, who once,
for our defunct *Literary Review*, wrote their piece?

Mr Vishnoodas replies:
Mumbai's Imtiaz & Anil Dharker – Duo Dharkers,
whose Nissim article threw the confetti of kindness.

Ms Gussama Beenon interjects:
Mr Alexander Pope, the beacon disability troubadour
(more so than even Lord Byron!) – who is not familiar
with his *Rape of the Lock*? It's said two family
lock horns in punga-munga, & Pope,
by jibberdy, an eye-watering satirist, was co-opt
to compose a kavya for smiling these wealthy
partisans into shanti. He then write his mock-haircut
Rape of the Lock. Pope profess that he write
his satire to laugh them all laughing back from pain.
Nissim compose to shoogle us also from pain.

Mr Vishnoodas concludes:
Irrefutably! Let this tale stand as allegory
to see if it can save this talkie from antics starting
which some may deem as shaming or savage vulgarity.

CHORUS:
Vulgar verse – what could harm
when Babu is painting the town laal?
But just now we're hearing howls
laughing with pleasure, plus howls
stonked with shock! Arrey whatwhat
is bloody tamasha!? To find out
if you deem scene unPC, please return
jaldi after sole ◄I§N√T»E¿R♥M▪IʃSiS✱I∧OʃN⊚~
which is presently decease soon-soon.

While ◄I§N√T»E¿R♥M∎IʃSiS✳I∧O¶N⊙~ gives our lungs
respite, we, the entire 50 CHORUS
would limelight that we've plumped,
throughout *indiom*, from the forms that polaris
our polymathic minds, for the Skaldic,
or the aura of such. Well, why not
share our preferred form like our
fellow poets – now that we're not cast,
as per norm, gaudy anomaly for laughout.

Nota bene, not 50, 42 of CHORUS is present
with eight in gridlock for weeks on their ascent
to crest of Charsovee – now stuck in bottleneck.

TRANSMISSIONS

CANTO

III

CANTO III

22

Rani Shakontala & neglected poets

On a poet with magical powers who recites a poem
about poets who failed because they relied on the
Queen's English, & images project from her stomach
which show old footage from a cafe in Mumbai

CHORUS:
Let us return now to the table, but antics?!
What antics? Arrey, but what the Dickens!
Next is Rani Shakontala with her Pwdin
Eva of a Welsh accent! Plus she spewing
        the acme of a human tum
        that put every Hottentot butt
        in a busted flush, is curved as
        Blumenbach's Caucasian skulls.

        Camera Operator whispers to Director:
Rani Shakontala Buddha belly is overhang
with adipose steeped in cholesterol & Type II syruping
through blood pressure
yet Rani Shakontala is residing on green prayer-
juice alone, solo. No apothecary, in perpetuity, requisite!
Plus on close inspection
                        she's
                        th
                        in
                        as a svelte teen,
            as that pickle temptress, Circe,

as Anna Pavlova, that swan of dying swans,
          who find even handstand scorpion
a cinch. How so? Rani Shakontala's every madam
          as in the parable of Gita, do by doing naught
          as by doing naught all's caught!

          Director replies:
Let's hear Rani Shakontala, whose honeyed score
soar high as Rabindranath Tagore's,
whose high-line was revived on Radio 4 Extra's
puissant & weekly *Poetry Extra*.

          Camera Operator:
Rani Shakontala seem to be above seat levitating
like the aerial suspension of the ancient Brahmins!

          While hovering above her seat, Rani Shakontala recites her poem about
          neglected poets because they did not write in Babu

please divert your route –
cease being up-hung on your journey end
with English by Queen,
or how you become Shakespearean fool
          (who vet self in real
time to question self) if self just hear Queen
          Queen Queen! ist godsend
if fool's critique ist a poem itself,
          its own micro-speak.

          ruck bolly to feel
spirit of branch-singing bird whose yellow
          dreams are like kella,
banana, whose essence we cannot peel,
ist rebel refrain of pure Princess Di –

yes yes Diana
whose kohl-Indic eyes beaut-box her sorrow!

who ist care the rickshaw driver we chide
      have asthmatic cough –
let him us deliver to chatterbox
      Irani cafe;
albeit hot as pastoral of Clough
      our non-Babu lays –
our POCs in the West are always waylaid,
      they're called copycat!

on my tum many scenes I ist enact
      & you must decide –
do I display satire of past brownnose
      or should we panegyre?
should we love or mock our love-mocked heroes.

Rani Shakontala floats, with chair beneath her,
to the apparent 'centre' of Bulbul Hall

CHORUS:
The screen is on the Rani's tum – she assemble
a device which is lit over her dress – a magic lantern,
      a prototype model.

In spiralling time-crescendos, all feel taken
to Mumbai, the cafe, the tall ceiling, the teak,
the punka, the tables thrummed with conversation.
All feel they're actually in Irani cafe. That Bulbul Hall
is thus transformed for Rani Shakontala's revelations.

She show Nissim offering feedback, his Papermate
hovering over hemp-rag paper of wunderkind Indic

poets. Then their young pages of verse sudden escape
out the cafe for downpour, for becoming wet wings
    that become alphabet soup
    for a sewer that's cock-a-hoop.
Dammit, whatnot & shucks, even Hopkin-Dickinson,
so why not Indic poets – survive early-door rejection.
Being FOR neither place, our poets are doom-nationed.

    Director, sobbing, says to Camera Operator:
Indian poets from India who write in English are not
desired by Ind. Thus they're drained by guilt, neglect.
What of the British poets, with the skin of India –
on what terms are they seen as a voice by Britannia.

*Director does not receive a reply & does not see the Camera Operator
assisting his camera team*

CHORUS:
Rani Shakontala – in the way a fairground mechanic
hushes his metropolis of generator machinery to kip,
so it is, Rani gives a beddy-bye to her magic lantern.
All feel returned to Bulbul Hall & the Rani's projection
remains upon her complicated tummy. She'll project
Babutopian visionaries in past or in crazy present.

23

Grand theorists & Mr S. T. Coleridge

Some grand theorists are viewed on tea cups, &
S. T. Coleridge, who behaves as though he's Vishnu
(having dreamt of being Vishnu when he was
mortal), is woken from his sleep in real-time Eternity

✸

*A series of cups which are upside-down float into Bulbul Hall from
the kitchen & move about over the heads of the poets*

CHORUS:
Collectorate are down on knees in orison
    at this strange Rani's prize-marrow
thin tum. Is her tum a Yeatsian gyre who'd pern
    parishioners in? Is she our

monkey god who'd open his own tum to disclose
    his pyar-amour for Rama?
Rani's tum has made a magicalamitous –
    look up, there, see how each bright star

has arrived in form of best value crockery
    cups   floating straight from the kitchen.
Each lit cup's now flipped upside-down, so chai empty
    over our stunned congregation?

No! Perhaps due to the firm milky skin each chai
    hold, hold so each skin show current
conduct in the universe, its circular time
    flash for us one heavenly event.

*Rani Shakontala shows some grand theorists when they were children
& already hard at work (Director is seen looking for the Camera Operator)*

Rani Shakontala raises her voice:
I'll ecstaticise in quintains
about our cosmic present-time,
    look – the shabash brilliant minds
in own room, yes, with candle flame.
    They're young, studying to create

a caboodle vision! All sat
    behind teeny desk donning cap
& plimsolls. Oh by blinking hell
    ist Johann & Friedrich Schlegel.
On another star/cuppa-skin,

    at it, Laura Riding Jackson.
There ist young – revolving far off –
    Edward Casaubon with his conk
at the keyhole of a theorem
    pleading for his golden key home!

*Rani Shakontala raises a hand at the ceiling, the room is dimly lit
but the Rani's face is visible to all*

Rani Shakontala says:
Look up at that upsy-down
    cuppa where a miracle
I will now execution,
    I ist write in an old style
to show a poet right now
    who I'll wake up – my vessel
of verse will be Mr Pound's
    mock-Chinese ideogram.
All kneel now at my goddam!

Look, a poet now sleeps
but I ist wake him to speak.

*Rani Shakontala raises a hand toward an upside-down cup (each cup is
actually as large as a five litre pot of paint), on the skin of the upside-down
cup a vision appears, the Rani speaks in Sanskrit & English*

Rani Shakontala says:
बराबर
in the spoken language of Sanskrit
I say what in Hindi at times I ist write

time	=	kālá
water	=	apa
dream	=	swapna
lotus flower	=	padma
circle	=	maṇḍala

संदर्भ
Mr S. T. Coleridge, ist he a German Romantic?
But he ist romanticising like a Jenna poetic –

a dream he write when in his mortal frame
which now he enact in death for all ages.

He ist with Indic accent on chai surface.
Why Indic? He act a god – he pay the price!

*S. T. Coleridge is on the thick tea-skin of a cup
& speaks to the poets in Sanskrit & English*

Mr Coleridge says:
दस लाख
'Greeting collectorate! I, Mr S. T.
Coleridge am. I like Vishnu am, I is furled sleep
in lotus flower

on TIME that is WATER.
Like god Vishnu, I wake for up-to two
        mins total after
1,000,000 year each time. Then I sleep duvet'd
        back in me
        padma.'

कमल

'You have seen me wake but know please
I'm in nirvana modality & made to peek
from lotus by Rani Shakontala – whom I endear.
But I must to sleep after two-mins for दस लाख.'

अभिज्ञानशाकुन्तलम्

'I endear Rani Shokantala. Once she was the star
in German Romantic theatre. Her lamb-like calm
for the classic Indic play Abhijnanashakuntala
that show all must return to the pre-industrial. Ta.'

*Having said his goodbyes, Mr Coleridge is heard
whispering the following ideograms*

शयन

'On the apa of kala in me padma
    for 1,000,000 back in a swapna
till Proto-Indo-Euro come full maṇḍala.
    Falalalaa   foldedol   falalala.'

अहिम्सा

'On the apa of kala in me padma
    for dasha lakhs back in a swapna
till Proto-Indo-Euro come full maṇḍala.
    Falalalaa   foldedol   falalala.'

Poets watch Mr Coleridge close his eyes, but then
he opens his eyes again & speaks drowsily

संस्कृत

'Mr Pound adored brush strokes for Mandarin,
I liebe the tantric scripting of Hindi for Sanskrit.'

Mr Coleridge has closed his eyes & is fast asleep inside his lotus flower
above the waters of time which are all visible on the tea-skin

24

Prayers to *The Golden Bough*

On a book that was influential in the West which now
inspires the poets to pray

❧

*The cups return to the kitchen, a book then hovers
above the heads of the poets*

Rani Shakontala says:

Enough ist of that enough, mine dear troubadours, the up-
side down cups I now remove to küche. What next I pop

in ceiling? By mine chakras, ist not best-sell Stephen Fry
Ode Less Travelled, though it do make each poet rhapsodise

into radical verse. Nor not the tales Ctesias made-
off from Ind named *The Indian Wonders* he spread in Med-

ieval Europe to ensure all troubadours overcome
their writing block. Ist rubricate tome, whose compendium

of spells bringing under one spire all that how-now-brown-
   cow
primitivity. Ist a kind of faith, our ark & plough

Sir J. G. Frazer 12 volume in 1 *The Golden Bough*.
Sir J. G. Frazer 12 volume in 1 *The Golden Bough*.

Our uomo universale! Our synkretistisch compote!
Yummy than best Babu-opus best-Babu ever wrote.

Rani Shakontala is still hovering centrally in the Hall with both arms raised

Rani Shakontala says to all:
Declaring I am, by & by, that all collectorate are
to fall weeping now on knees 'neath its geek force,
all ist chant prayer while *The Golden Bough* soar
Bulbul Hall like bullion in the brill air.

*(The Golden Bough hovers high up in Bulbul Hall; the poets,
camera crew & chorus fall in prayer beneath it; each group recites
a section of the prayer which is divided into three parts)*

Ode to *The Golden Bough*

You have make the world more glassy than glass,
you are bright than glass, you are colour more tropic
than glass – more telescopic than glass!
You have annealed our mortal plot
lo! glass where everyone's flesh,
the heart's low swinging chariot
must find own heaven as it lift
past the dance of
sphere on sphere
spinning top
stellar bop
Lindy Hop!

All had fallen into a falsetto for the final line of the prayer

25

Indian road signs

On the joy of Indian road signs, & an invitation for
the reader of the book version

ᴗ

CHORUS:
Director is not praying but looks stunned
by this act of unisonance, this recitation
& fellowship as in a national anthem.
Director assumed he was ordering
into action the Camera Operator till
he sees that the Operator is also on his knees, up
& down flapping before that Olympian thin-tum.

Director drags the Camera Operator up from the floor

Director whispers to Camera Operator:
What is this bondoogle, this hot water excess!?
Are we playing to the gallery as *Satanic Verses*
& suchlike who make savages of Indic faiths?
Must all minorities be exfoliated by shame?
Or are we so settled in the West that the time's
arrived for our Achilles Heels to be satirised?

Camera Operator momentarily turns to his back pocket to stare
at the smile of Mr Dante in purgatory

Camera Operator distracts Director:
While our troubadours finish their orison

I'll play Public Information Broadcast on screen
of Indian road signs which are educative
about correct conduct. They also have vim
& Promethean candelabra of Babalarium!

Director, pleased, replies:
Road signs are turbocharged craic, Operator!
I will leave in the folio a box for inspired
readers to create their own bold road signs –
perhaps about driving in hurry for curry
or to alleviate a fast approaching Delhi belly!

Camera Operator:
Noting if they're inside or outside our culture
is determining the politicality of their humour.

CHORUS:
Please use space below to create own road sign,
with giddy limits of tonal correctitude in mind.

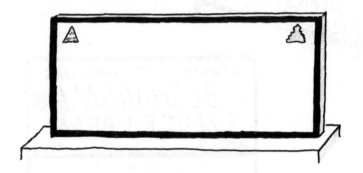

Camera Operator whispers to Director:
Poets scream, chungars! What through ceiling,
        that is entrance door, is ad absurdum pass
        in!
Is a Grendelian Angelina Jolie freak!
        Is she in wrong talkie? This is not Mead
        of Hrothgar – what if she's in feed mood!?

26

Geordie lass makes observations

On some suggestions about the real purpose of in-
diom, & finding one's own voice

Footsteps are heard about Bulbul Hall

Director says to Camera Operator:
Door opens for a damsel   in Newcastle football
kameez. She's in the room.   Despite the cut-up floors
she's like magician's helper   who has been sawed
& seem halved, in two cut   boxes, staggered walk.

Camera Operator replies:
No monster – an Ali Baba troving our Xanadu cave,
excepting she speak a pure Geordie for which we paid
a translator to make her muckawucka plain.
Sorry to say, the translator is my aunt, she's from
Sunderland. Standard English is not her foremost
lingo. She tried her best to simplify what Geordie is say.

Director replies:
Geordie lass dawdles in trainers. She loves her
soccer team so much she wears their kit. Unlike all
top wealthy clubs – her team never lost their soul,
were never sport-washed by a shonky investor.

Camera Operator replies:
As she dawdle about – her skin, in the axed

refractions of light have many shades. Who'd
simplify her subtlety as 'choc. complexioned'!?

     Geordie lass says to the collectorate:

Hwaet! in *Monsters,* Inc. they've magic
doors wot flip ye reet foreign.
I swung me door in, in a sec
I was owa n oot. Me in yer wacky
room fer this flick! From me laptop
I were watchin yer wazzock racket
till I licked a ken, at school the lads ll
take the rip when you roll these odd
beats of Bharat thought, they'll mock em
in class in me face, when ye fake these voices
it's me wot picks up the pieces, but then
I ken – I'll outwit em! Here's me quest,
me tongue's bricked in me brain, so how
do I, like James Joyce – hear me
meself, to see it, to see me own patter?
Ah, to be meself! Yer talkie might
help me brekk out fer gobbin me brown
skin-like lingo. Haddaway, soz,
I'm bad fer disruptin yer beltin flick.

Ye must be confused why I've crashed in –
is there a design to this diction you do,
this multy-kulty? I can't mek out
if it prods a viewer's unconscious to probe
the barometer of their learning – to backchat
their rank constructs, like rinsing the face
to watch the dirt gluggin the drain.
Oh nee, me views I'm always voicin em.
I'm a reet cackhouse. I'll shut me crud.

Geordie lass in flapping stripey shirt
is walking about the Hall emboldened
by the smiley poets who enjoy her turn,
she is being recorded till she go home.

Geordie lass says:
What if the *Monsters, Inc.* door int magic
but summit deep: if it's dualistic?
In that flick, monsters step though a factory
door into bedrooms of bairns sleepin.
They scare these kiddies to mek em scream;
these screams are turned to energy, how smart!
These screams power the sunny metropolis.
But the monsters learn that larks are best
to win em charge, so when they womble
in a kiddie room & mek raspberries
& laughs, they mek the metropolis leccy!

Now yer flick, it's like *Monsters* flick
I reckon yer gods come down to gad
on earth, to test ideals. Yer totally
at it, in mortal make-up fer leela.
Leela's the divine play of the deities,
yer at it revealin to folks revelations –
the fabulate festival, the universe at frolics.
I know me stuff! Yer here to suss out
through talkie, yer here to test,
what if Babu's the gob best gabbed by folk.
It's yer gomen, right, then you'll be gone
to heaven havin given us a happy
insight in leela. Nee, nee, leave off
I'm grouchin crud! I'll shut me cakehole.

Poets recognise Geordie teen's parasocial
interaction. They applaud so much that she feel,
or at least looks it – silvery-lit on screen.

Geordie lass says:

Ye clappin me, pet?	Can't be. Ye laughin
at me? Am I played?	Back at primary school
Miss Brodie sneaked in	that paisley scholar,
ye heard him, Michael	Foucault. His hetero
topia. Well he	talked of the migrant
mekin the lingo	renewed thru the licks
& leaps of the flesh,	the flesh he reckons
the tool which toys	with the native talk
to save it from	reet old soppiness.
The old with the new	opens the door
to a brand new stott.	From stale to stott
or else lingo moves	too slow from likeness.
Ye get me, but if	yer gods, you don't need
me to say aught.	Oh eck. I'm stale
not stott, I'm talking	tosh! I'm sorry.

Director whispers to Camera Operator:
Committee stand, are moving to the girl –
she can't halt talking. In Dostoevsky's *The Double*,
the protagonist is alone at a party & is ushered out.
Our collectorate, like all Indians, ♥ Dostoevsky. Albeit
lovingly – they hug the Geordie lass. Ah, it amends
the heart to see their group hug which is held
a sizeable while from above & beneath.
Our Geordie lass seems moved to tears.

Camera Operator replies:
She's happiest, for certs, amid this inbetweenness.

Is why she's reduced to a Keatsian stoop
as she elevate a bruised wrist for the brass
handle leading her to her bedroom
which she share with two older bros.

　　　Director interrupts:
Before she departs *Monsters Inc.*-ingly
through her door to her hell, purgatory
or paradise – catch the end of her oratory!

Before closing her bedroom door, the Geordie lass whispers,
with two fingers raised in salute, the mantra which she extends
by echoing Mr Thomas Babington Macaulay

'Know thy Blighty, know thy Blighty.
Long live our shelf of Euro library.'

27

Mrs Dai Pitta's writing activity

On a writing exercise that could send all the poets
home in an instant, & making connections with
place

〜

Mrs Dai Pitta is invited to speak & does so in her Welsh accent

'Bore da, or is it good evening? Anyhow, Mr Vishnoodas
I feel quelled as a kebab spit that is revolving
to beget a juicy kebab as I wonder how that lass
revolved doors for home. I've an idea through verse,
of how to scoot home, in the Welsh form of Gwawdodyn.
May I confess, I am from Wales, nowadays bereft
of dreams in Hindi, dreaming only in Welsh.

Mr Desani says to Mrs Dai Pitta:
I dream in the Greek, most often as a prancing dryad.
But please tell, what if poets channel cydymdreiddiad,
can they return home? That if the artist & their homeland
interpenetrate, they can become their own fountainhead.

Mrs Dai Pitta agrees:
Dda! When a poet can embrace cydymdreiddiad,
they can teleport home. When artist & homeland
interpenetrate, they become own fountainhead!

CHORUS:
Confused a tad, dear viewer, by that chat?

Cydymdreiddiad is Welsh concept of place
& poet as one, the grafting occurs if a poet
can express place within own true voice.
This expression can be figurative description
or implicit in the deep qualia of articulation.
Still confused? When you feel that profound
Welsh nexus – enjoy your cydymdreiddiad!

Mrs Dai Pitta blushes at the attention from Mr Desani,
then faces the poets to recite her poem

Hotty botty! jiw jiw! As I fondle
my leek brooch – so there's a swmpus portal
to slip me back to Lassi Wood? To act
in a play – my part? I'm play a Welsh lass.

That toon saved time with a *Monsters, Inc.* door.
Friends, let us codi our pens. Let us pour
our hearts in song. Yes, when hometime bell's bong
we'll fly through our lay in a popty-ping!

CHORUS:
Each poet is now writing their poem
which will have the power to zap them home.
In silence, each poet's lost to the activity
with Bablish poets going lingotastic –
not even seeing page they swoosh
as if with the quill of Jane Austen
who said she composes on her 'two
inches of ivory with so fine a brush'.
Plus also – Coolie poets are caught in
oral prints in the cerebrum. No rush.

Camera Operator to Director:
Poets have been writing for prolong

period, notwithstanding a poem being writ, is it not,
when at workshop, done & dusted, in 20,
in 20 Circadian? Not 20 league!?

    Director replies:
Yet when was a poem ever composed
that, on recital, it can at-once teleport
the poet of the poesy – home sweet home!?
True home comes when poet's at true disport.

    CHORUS:
Mrs Dai Pitta has constructed an aromapoem
à la Eduardo Kac, by lacing a page with her home
fragrances. Dai Pitta's aromapoem is of course
wordless. A molecular poem best read by the nose,
    sniff, sniff! But is best
    no one sniff too breakneck
suggests Mrs Dai Pitta, or be derailed,
summarily sent to madcap Laugharne in Wales.

28

Ms Kuku Paku & ringtone saga

On three Greek masks, a poem about Wordsworth's
Lucy & Ms Kuku Paku at a picnic, & the impact of a
phone ringtone

All poets pass around Mrs Dai Pitta's poem to smell it

Ms Kuku Paku, gently sniffing, says:
My nose is jumping, Mrs Dai Pitta – your poem
is a fragrant link to my own lay about home.
I must compose my own aromapoem hereafter!
Till then, please, my dear troubadours I hope
we can agree, jagde da lakh/suttee da kakh,
only the perky will ease the world off their back.
Here's a glossary to help explain the barter
     in my Rispetto lay. Kosh is gay,
       desh is nation, & panee's for lake.

To add, I will now raise to my features
my mask for Greek god Momus whose satire's
so benign it have the praise of panegyre.
Yet one error is frequent with my masks, haihai!
When I hold before my face for my speaking part,
for the horror of humour, my comedic Momus mask
turns out is my mask for Thalia, perhaps, unknown
is even tragic mask of Melpomene!? A miscalculation
when I cannot decipher anymore which disguise
is for which – my masks don the same nervous smile!

Ms Kuku Paku recites her Rispetto
with a mask in front of her face

I would picnic on nostalgia for our desh
of Allah-Vishnu, yet also I am kosh
to parkrun a windy prelude at Grasmere
while at sahib Wordmirth's ebbed inland panee.

Distracted by his Simpliciad, I'd cry,
'Ai Lucy, getting up! The rocks I've unroll
off your bod so on this sunny hillside
let's feast the chutney of Mr Ezekiel.'

After applause, Mrs Dai Pitta says:
Syndod! Ms Kuku – as you read your poem 'to return
you home', you were nearly vanish homeward
were my grist not for gripping your ankles earthward!

Ms Kuku Paku replies:
I was disappearing-reappearing! What sojourns
& journeys this poetry-moiety have in provisions.

CHORUS:
Ms Kuku Paku phone's gone jhil mill gaudy. A racket
issues from her ring tone – it will not reticent!
Her popular tune ringtone is recurrent.

Extract of song playing from Ms Kuku Paku's phone is 'Ddu-Zu
Ddu-Zu' by BlackPinkBarnes, a pop band who engage
the Dorset of William Barnes with K-Pop

CHORUS:
jom doaky nan hodmadod
you koaky me you getting quob

oh wait till we yop to the bandy
oh wait till we lisom in the parrick

hit you with that ddu-zu-zu-zu ddu-zu-zu-zu
      you're my honey-zuk!

     Camera Operator whispers to Director:
The song is keep repeating, Ms Kuku Paku is perplexing.
Apache Brummy – will he end the career of this ring

     cycle. He has leapt & is swing-
     ing via a light cord, back-flipped into the pit

where is seated Mr Desani, then he's somersaulted across
several depressions & floors aquaplaning on the impress

     of poetic hands that heave along Apache to a stop
     so he thunderbolt –

CHORUS:
hit you with that ddu-zu-zu-zu ddu-zu-zu-zu
     you're my honey-zuk!

     Camera Operator whispers to Director:
Apache is thunderbolt his little left finger
packed with gold rings
toward Ms Kuku Paku's Samsung.

     Director replies:
Indeed, Ms Kuku Paku, for the whole stretch,
have her phone held above her bun-head,

thus Brummy, while air-leapt, he locate
& fastidiously press, having taken leave of personal cost

to anatomy, even biro behind ear, while falling on
a kind of mezzanine still in one fantabulous form –

CHORUS:
hit you with that ddu-zu-zu-zu ddu-zu-zu-zu
        you're my honey-zuk!

Director continues:
One form to make his hot shot for our epyllion, by what
is meant, he press on that delinquent phone, MUTE.

> *Ms Kuku Paku joins the applause from all the poets*
> *while changing the mask in front of her face,*
> *which looks identical to the previous mask*

Ms Kuku Paku says:
You know, my grand-daughter, Maia is K-pop
bonkers that she set, prior to our workshop,
my ringtone to tease my want of technology.

> *Apachi Brummy picks up from the floor his pink biro*
> *which had fallen from behind his left ear*

29

Mr Kumbarkarn's infelicity

On Sir Vidiadhar Surajprasad Naipaul's exploitation
of Indians, & a whimsy on three writers of colour
who lived in Wiltshire at the same time

Mr Kumbarkarn, standing, says to all:
Forsooth, aye, I am hippopotamusly humongous!
I chew Hudibrastics, weasels & raison d'être
down in my hut on Gokarna Beach! Then I rumpus
with my mastiff bitch to K-pop! I make my shelter
amid *Indo sapiens*. Yet a literary god is one whom
I find's a backassward. Hear my Judas/Janus poem
which I muck-about in the mandakranta metre.

Mr Kumbarkarn is still standing
as he recites his poem

Buffeted we've been by the poetics of place – so let me
      invoke
one who is feet first in the stocks, called, Mr V. S. Nightfall –
      who when
the stooping world-over Browndom was at his brogues
      & keen to hallow
him a home in their nation, he opt instead to homify
      Stonehenge!

Pomped with knighthood amid the gentry, he came false-
      circle by slopping

at our faces the fairground sponge just to win the Blighty
        accolades!
Was this pussycat-fedora man refreshing bolly through
        Indic
folklore or race folktalk!? White sepulchre, mimic man,
        Merlin's lackey!

*Chorus will imagine a scenario where two famous authors who actually
lived near each other have a third, a Babu poet, living nearby*

CHORUS:
Collectorate do 'awkward turtle' with their hands,
owing to 'bitter' tone of Mr Kumbarkarn.
Sepia coloured photos are on screen for a flashback
that is now about to spin its curious yarn
featuring Mr Vikram Seth, Mr V. S. Naipaul
& a mighty peer who's presently at Bulbul Hall!

So, the yarn. As one word is remote yet
somehow vicinal to another – let's note
Mr Vikram Seth had up-sticks for a belle-
vie in Wiltshire, ever so nigh his beau
idéal, Mr Naipaul. Two Indics retreat
to same shire is inspired! Unbeknownest
to Ind (Mr Naipaul would not meet
or greet this Mr Seth), accompanied
by his batman & in double-breasted
pin-stripes, if we could Adam & Eve
such a conceit, 'twas our chap of belles-
lettres – Mr Vishnoodas, who'd abode
within earshot, almost of Mr Seth.
Did their triumvirate paths for an iota,
ever – no, not met even for a shadow!

Save that Mr Vishnoodas had once been to egress
a par avion in a Salisbury missive box – a body swivel
after Mr Seth posted at the same elephantiasis of red.
Both being amiss their peer had precipitated a missal.
Genius, a mower in the lonesome glow-worm of a dell
        when authors from the same cot of heritage
        never suckle same nipple for mutual milk.

*Mr Vishnoodas walks in Mr Kumbarkarn's shadow as he
approaches him about Mr Naipaul*

        Mr Vishnoodas, boldly, says:
Pecksniffian? Why, Sir, you are the most high-built,
plus too, you are almost the most excelsior erected
with your Mumbai condos. I say – is there a benefit
you've had deficit? Babu's our act for asset.

        Mr Kumbarkarn, smiling, replies:
Forsooth, aye, Mr Vishnoodas – I admit I'm Larry
happy with Mr Nightfall's mischief. His cunnery.

*Camera turns to Mr Common Man, who is whispering
to Ms Gussama Beenon*

        Mr Common Man says:
Did not Mr Kumbarkarn say his recitation
was in the mandakranta metre – as you will notion,
is called the 'slow lady approaching' metre,
the saucy form for the 'slow stepper'.

*Ms Gussama Beenon is seen counting the syllables of her poem,
in a classic style, that she has just written*

    Ms Gussama Beenon replies:
Hai! Now we see who's making
'the slow step'. Mr D is
touching Mr K's shoulder
soft as touching gossamer.
Their double burra men-shape
have hulk the Hall with shade
as they are falling into
a kiss of pukka repute,
that we may be blunt to say,
as a spade is called a spade,
they're in an osculation
of anacreontic grade!

Mr Common Man & Ms Gussama Beenon are seen laughing while
everyone else looks away from the sight of yet another kiss in the talkie

30

Cricket ball

On a cricket ball being heard

A cricket ball from 20-20 falls up from the floor

for the ceiling about the astrolabe chandeliers – we hear

its crunching sound as though it's rolling over white marks painted on grass

CANTO

IV

CANTO

IV

31

Poets attempt atavism

On a dance postponed, & poets in a trance & appear-
ing to return to their own native languages

Camera Operator whispers to Director:
The majesty motion of the cricket ball is excited
the collectorate causing their limbering
    to broom the bones, to wow
        the junctures, the doolally Hall hollows
        with a bhangra or lavani transport
to an underground fusion classic, 'Boundrry! Boundrry!
Hawk-Eye Boundrry!' by the Googly Brothers.

Extract of the song is performed by chorus while poets appear
to be warming up for some dancing

CHORUS:
(hoh hoh) baby why you hit the ball too feist
see it (hoh hoh) hot the head of a migrant
who was swimming on the (hoh hoh) line

do we bang-bang-bhangra for the new cricket
do we bang-bang-bhangra for the old cricket
push the boundary back to Krypton
keep it tight as a rope at the Oval

arrey boundrry boundrry-ee
bastards Hawk-Eye boundrry-ee

chukk Punjabi bales for the 20-20
chukk Punjabi bales for the 40-40

or sit on your butt for the red ball
that's the red ball of brown hell
arrey boundrry boundrry-ee
bastards Hawk-Eye boundrry-ee

all the brothers & the sisters in the house
chukk your arms in the air giving shout:

cow-corner in-ducker duck hit-the-deck
grubber leg-cutter teapot good-length
lollipop nick-&-nurdle sledging stonewall
chin-music bend-your-back Bunsen dead-ball

Poets cease preparing to dance & fall onto their knees & into a trance

Camera Operator whispers to Director:
But   but   but   what the what!!!
Poets are all succumbing for the floor by their seat.
Each is fallen on one or two knee.
Each is on knee *but* fast asleep, like a tuk tuk
etherised in a ginnel with punctured honker.

Director replies:
From the knee-fall they are being wrought.
Each poet's being wrought by some anti-Babu
        mental software virus reboooot.
In the reboot – can they be made pure-tongue, as in yore,
a pedigree, a saaf baaj, clean jeeb tongue, not bhaji-glot!
Let's focus on their Titanic quest to return to their native
lingos – with zero English on their tongues to report.
CHORUS will recite, for folio, their attempt at atavism.

*Poets are on their knees with their eyes closed, they tilt sideways,
this way then that, at the same time, as though some interior jolt
has occurred in their bodies*

CHORUS:
A sober light like a whack –
a sheen making everyone blink,
jolt like a ship crash at an iceberg's hardcore neck!

Everyone blinking for sight
but when sight eventually settle
each tongue feel dumpty heavy after iceberg spat.

Each is find their Bab-
u tongue is not on tap.
What's dripping from the historical vessel we call the trap

is neither Babu, not Coolie,
is nativistic speech!
Each is flailing to stay euphonic but they screech,

screech like a packet of limbs waving over the sea,
yet on they flail through this payar metre. Ah, payar means

love, in this other jeeb. Not time for love when each frozen
wash up poet is jab the jeeb as suit their complexion.

here lies one who abandon his mum
if you whiff his tongue is wazzed-on mud

One sputtering Konkani – one drowning
by Urdu kept
rhyming. Do you think they understood
their fellow? No, not

a stroke! Do you think they know what
            has rowed from their mouth?
No, not a stroke! Their mouth row on like a
            swimmer gone south

while the brain is been ejected – bummed
            on a hard shoulder.
Each watched its mouth drive on driverless
            facing its neighbour.

                    here lies one is grump & lonely
                    who in himself not ever agree

            Each feel it last a year
without winter in this custom.
            Each tried chit-chat is like a child
running for the bosom

            of a mother but always missed –
falling instead in our
            Gandhi saltpit. Mumma is wanted,
not salt! Their lids are

            lifted. But. But they are unconscious, the trauma
            bombshell –
            each must keep at knee till is passing by
                    Mr Brunel
            rescue service, SS *Great Britain*! It saves all,
                    or, or

            wait it out for ancestors on blinking boat
                    with no oar!?

                    here lies one dishonoured with fame
                    for desi-crating his own surname

Poor ancestral pop-up
attacks the unconscious icecap
known as each poet's id, till they're shamed off the Indo map.

Let's melt this iceberg lineage,
melting this bizarre image
bizarre as albatross speaking Gullah, for its dockage.

Poets remain slumped by their seats

Director says to Camera Operator:
Move cameras elsewhere till committee have disen-
cumbered from that dye-in-the-wool Brobdingnagian
vehicle – the native tongue; that national strain.

32

Advert for Hindi

On how Hindi should be the language of India rather
than English

～

CHORUS:
ADVERT for Hindi Bindi Board is played for talkie
audience only,
      in a split-screen two men are seen,
      a Coolie chef & milk delivery man.
      They are on rotary-dial handset;
      dood, milk, is not delivered, chef
      & dood man have dissimilar accent,
      in dog eat dog this talk's inefficient
      (our Sunderland translator has 'cleansed'
      obscure lingo for maximus sense).

On the screens, facing the poets, an advert is played

chef	kee I do-do with blooting, mister?
milkman	the dood is good, is it?
chef	is ney dood, baba, is blooting
milkman	I see, I see, is it?
che	kee do you for blooting?
mil	the dood roll from gaddee, is it?

        [keening cow keen for milking,
        is seen behind milkman who is ignoring]

che	no mister! Dood eat sun onnu-randu clock
mil	pukka, green, cream, is it?
che	blooting of reeking, mister
mil	is post-gone, I new bring, is it
che	or cheque blooting mister

CHORUS:
In freeze-frame, both men bear the sheaves
of behemoth moustache, the soggy heat
     in which they hold
     the confusing phone.
Before them, a petite man with a red swasti
on his forehead is seen in middle of screen-split.
Swasti man's moustache is long & fine as the hook blade
held aloft by demented Kali. He will parade
his nationalist ideals broken on some horse & cart
couplets – an odd choice for our literally highbrow sirdar!
     He speaks in the Cywydd Deuair Hirion,
     is not a Hindi form but from the Welsh tradition
     he'll use it to mock the Coolie chef & milkman.

Swasti man is seen on the screen

Crore namaste; good in't it.
crore namaste, sound thrilling!

     [He laugh while drinking,
     Hindi-script is on can drink.]

It mean 10 million hell-
os; in English is messy.

Yes, you agree, it is clean
in Hindi, in our nation.

Now, that phone call, it was slow
like a tongue whose day's over.

Is slow when we blow hot-cold
with these Englo-soiled lingos.

> [He laugh while drinking,
> Hindi-script is on can drink.]

Their lingos were far in part
as, let's say, the partition

between Esperanto &
Ba Ba Black Sheep. Chat quicksand!

Trade sunk, when identikit
transaction not be meeting.

Our great leader speak Hindi
only, the path for the free.

Come home! Hindi is fundoo,
fundoo mean cool, for cool dood!

> [He laugh while drinking,
> Hindi-script is on can drink.]

*Silence after the advert; the main table is one large table yet it, as ever,
appears to be a series of desks behind which each sleeping poet is seated*

Camera Operator says to Director:
Many poets are escutcheoned in a panda landscape
of nod while inwardly still on their travails
with their Mr Virgil. Their heads droop off their escritoire.
But why is each depth of desk 18 inches mere?

Director, standing over Common Man, says:
To match the desk Emily Dickinson made her omphalos,
the volcano for her eruptus. Her size brings all godsend.
Know thy Blighty.

Camera Operator replies:
Know thy Blighty.

Some time has passed & the poets are still in a trance or fast asleep

Director pulls aside the production team:
A talkie cannot survive by expedition of snooze.
It requires surplus humour. Let's hire without ado
those American sitcom big guns. You know, Raj
Koothrapalli, from *Theory of Big Bang*,
& *Van Wilder*'s Taj Badalandabad?
Pigeon-chested, wet mummy boys. A blast
for laughout when they palaver Babu.

Production Manager replies:
Taj & Raj? Boy! You not hear. They're nonplussed. When
leaving, you know, off-set – they stilllll parley Babu.
Their fanbase is happy? No, grousing! *Hey!what!the!heck!*
that your real speak, dude? Was gonna buy your merch, dude!
What next? All are monk-dumb. Gone straight-face off-set,
cos off- or on-camera, how's it – Raj-Taj they're the same
Babu voice all day? Yes! *The same!* Subject not to change!
Reification? No! Deification? No! Anti-deification? You bet.

Production Manager pulls out a pen & draws
five perfect smiles on the Director's folio

Production Manager continues:
Hey, boss, your folio – I ramp it with five smile test!
Distract reader with test! What else!? If they detest

our humour & colour zero smiles, let them chomp at
the publisher's bit – *arrey Fibber of Fibber, cheque back!*

colour-in smiles indicating current relish with *indiom*

low relish, low smile

high relish, high smile

cheque back

keeping cheque

33

The Babu of Mrs Japprey

On littlebloods who come to awaken the poets, &
Babu as a language suited to serious thought, & the
limits of satire

〰

Director whispers to Camera Operator:
Poets are all awoken by a posse
      of cutey-pie
littlebloods, created by Mr Hughes, poet.
      You know them – size
of fruit fly with Ganesha-like proboscis.
      How do they wake
each poet? By rousing their conscience
      for an empire heroic.

Camera Operator replies:
As each poet is wake to be on seat again,
      they seem at first
groggy as a phalanx of 'red Indians'
      on a reed boat
who haul their cargo of one alligator
      in a Tarzan
talkie. Tell me please, how are poets
      fully woken?

Director:
By singing a poem! Today is a tune
      every Babu, in Raj,

committed to heart – it's 'Casabianca',
     the boy stood on the burning deck
     whence all but he had fled.

     Camera Operator:
In my very bones is that tune;
yet beautiful & bright he stood,
as born for the storm he'll rule.

     Director:
The light in the room has adopted a puckish mien
seeming teenily crittered by golden flecks when
littlebloods, having crooned, are chull-chulling away
for a field of green roses, green in the shade.
     Bye bye cutey-pie littlebloods.
     Bye bye cutey-pie littlebloods.

As littlebloods fly out of the window, they are heard whispering to the poets

bye.bye.babus.coolies–baboolies

CHORUS:
Littlebloods return to sporting field where is comp
between medley centaurs, 'corns, goblins
griffins, refereed by Papa Toothwort in cloudless
roof playing Quidd – No, stop! Of late, the authoress
with daemon powers to intrepid this game been
shit-showed; best be craven, snip-off this scene!

Director says to Camera Operator:
Cameras to the quick! Mrs Japprey's about to recite
her Skeltonic verse. Her voice fills me with the sight
of a veiled-lady mushroom. She'll consider if Babu
can be a good language for the formal mood.

Mrs Japprey stands & recites her poem in the Englyn Byr Cwca form

Could Babu soften each note –
even jazz hands desist their daily clamour
while thought becomes quiet

quiet so Babu can sigh
her gravitas so refined she rushes
even war for ceasefire

ceasefire of the pulpit so
Word on-high blow the fogs congregating
a funeral widow?

OR widow-wailing it's grooved
for the bang sassatudes of a Mumbai
dhol dholing dhoom dhoom dhoom!?

Director addresses Director's Assistant:
Babu is capable of satire but we must desist
for our society lady, Mrs Japprey.
She is fringed by cultural codes, so cannot resist
the supercilious politesse of her community.
If the chucked tomato of satire begins – if it begins,
it must be wiped off because cherry picking
a value apart from the vast grocery of values,
a person lives harvested in, is, baldly – bad fruit.

Director's Assistant has a half-shaved head:
Satire will weaponise the offended to seek libel.
Easier to bear the shield of izzat by reinscribing
this chock-block talkie as a praise lay, a panegyre.

Director replies to Director's Assistant:
Mrs Japprey stands crash-hot, head over height,
bobbing like Blackpool lights. Wowsers to her bright
breeches with their spangled lace plus waistcoat.
She's of course for the occasion a molly, that is,
yes, a cross-dress queer from age of Macaroni.

Director now whispers to Camera Operator:
She's like Mary, wedding bells, Hamilton, from previous.
Macaronics are a fitting cut for mention of *Ulysses*.
Why, it's June, & it's Bloomsday – a day of wild carouse.
For which I believe Mrs Japprey will contravene
hidebound rules to serve us her sui generis cuisine.

Mr Desani has been addressing Mrs Jappery:
Why Mrs Japprey, from the vulcan
stithy of your kitchen you plate
Bangkok fare to Fat Duck fusion –
pure lingua franca pies piping hot.

Of recent – you flew abroad yet today
you present us C18th tucker –
macaroni pie! What an age when zany
off-piste fashions were de rigueur.

I hear these assorted pies are a mix
of Indic-Irish to celebrate Bloomsday –
mosquito gravy & lamb kidneys,
Bombay Duck in mutton veins.

Ivory vowels crusted with 'Rotten
English' reveal that you're our spiritus
mundi. Mrs Japprey's the emblem
of Babu who feed us devilled umbilicus!

CHORUS:
Mention of Rotten English & all fall-in for the king
of Rotten Mash – red-cap Ken Saro-Wiwa, was hang
quarter century past for speaking to the rot.
How do all fall in? Like the blackbird of Adlestrop –
'for that minute it sang', as though a minute were
commemoration, memorial enough for the rear
view of loss & the post-view of change. So it was
our crew applaud Saro-Wiwa; nota bene, pure applause
(unlike new-style footie kick-off claps plus boos).

  Director whispers to Camera Operator:
Mr Desani's address, I fear, was laced with
satire for Mrs Japprey. He was tunking out his
bovver boots! I hope our inestimable dame
will now scoop her mocked prerogatives from
under those goonda feet! The super-privilege
from birth must still adjudicate on polemical
conduct. Conduct such as gender, ableism, race
for which they will don blindfolded scales of justice.
If ever the likes of Mrs Japprey are not always P
C they would never be nettled by an angry
mob to not apologise – to not act they're martyred.
Or have we, I say, bombaclot the value of old blood.

  Camera Operator, confused, replies:
I endear how the tones of Babu must oscillate,
but, I say, what you say is tonally extortionate!
You been domiciled offshore from Ind too long, your tone

is uncertain to me. Are you the earnest OTT notes
of Ind or the sark & irony of the West? Any case,
I hear Mrs Japprey will bestow us the landay,
the Afghan couplet humble what she enunciate.

34

Mrs Japprey & East/West engagements

On attitudes of the 'West' to the 'East' as epitomised
by famous chefs & their fusion dishes, & an ungrate-
ful servant

Mrs Japprey ceases wiping her eyes for Ken Saro-Wiwa,
then recites her poem which is addressed to Mr Desani

My Sir, is agreed I'm an oddbod –
true too I am rich as a third world treasury pot.

By instinct, I'm a badge wearing New
Interculturalist – while Euro

Chef aeroplanes to Eastern backyard
for a day, then is back on telly with fusion blend –

a flish dish – on whose terms is that flish?
Surely it's an imperially imbalanced fusion.

I'll be on the box with my mockery
of *Lucky Cat* – Gordon Ramsay's fusion of East–West.

When the oven door purrs ope, my pies,
my octagonal Macaronis will blow mindsets.

Smell, how for construct validity –
each Macaroni pie has a honk of Billingsgate!

Apachi Brummy is knitting a design with Ms Homi Bibi, the latter
simply enjoys hearing her fellow & smiles along to his comments

Apachi Brummy whispers to Ms Homi Bibi:
Ho dis East–West ruckus, it's da same as rap –
when a bruv slick a jazz line on da rap beats
he claim his jam is a fusion! Ho! Dere's no jazz
heritage cuttin' da vinyl – it's still a rap track!

Camera Operator whispers to Director:
Who is mocking or being mocked now, in truth,
Mrs Japprey servant has entered wearing a loincloth
to the bellybutton, elsewhere he is caught short!

Mrs Japprey sighs then squints at her servant to speak,
her servant addresses the poets

Ebry   tom

        dick   ov

                harry

        pleej   eeeat.

Poets seem outraged & are heard mumbling

Mr Desani, in verse libre:
What is this hari-kari, this eructation! If I'm not mistaken
Mrs Japprey, your servant
        has just uttered Tom, Dick & Harry,
a most aspirational idiom, as Rob, Dock & Bury.

Ms Begum Jaan heard a ruder form of address than Mr Desani suggested

Ms Begum Jaan whispers to Kutcha Butcha:
Me not hear only Rob, Dock, Bury. Too
me hear this Gungadin say Nob, Prick
of Willy! This Coolie 'shark' – he's a tack!
His three words bishbosh the Raj, also Babu!
Three meanings by servant – all is shouting clear
to us Coolie, can Babu ever feel it to hear?

Kutcha Butcha replies:
Ipso facto – sound & sense are tectonic,
thus any layer of phonic or semantic
can consanguineously coexist.

Ms Begum Jaan is confused by his words:
What is yoo say with yor big boll?
Yet me like yor boll – its honky tonk.

Director whispers to Camera Operator:
Poor Mrs Japprey is red as a rugby scrum of rubbed
cheeks. Yet is erect, an upright molly, albeit in a huff
that her servant has embarrassed her so much.

Mrs Japprey says to Mr Vishnoodas:
Mr Desani, I apologise most meekly. My lackey – I instil
the *OED* in him, his profit's to profane. Or being idiot
to a genius ordinance, he'll never navigate our diction.
He declare names such as Tom & Dick are impossible
for the 'program' of his tongue-muscle to mollycoddle.
I'll hear him in kitchen, slicing reindeer-sushi, toying
with these skeuomorph, robot sounds, for chopping
& suchlike. He is, for certs – a Coolie beatbox.

Mr Desani offers consolation:
You fly this maschinenmensch amid your celebrity,

endowing wings to one for whom the gutter was starry.
Cuisine fames yet unenlightens this, this mechanism.
How bottomless your fame if freed from this altruism.

     Director whispers to Camera Operator:
To impress our poets, Mrs Japprey is asking
her servant to sing his ditty. She must regard
this Coolie as more than a dutiful dullard.

     Mrs Japprey instructs her servant:
Servant! Eeder chull!
Ek dum. Tu boll
tumka song. Chull chull!

35

Sound poem by Mrs Japprey's servant

On a sound poem that might be a Marxist cry from
the starved, the significance of a servant in a talkie,
& how the talkie might be more a panegyre than a
satire

*Servant enters on being asked to recite his own poem
inspired by Kurt Schwitters's 'Ursonate'*

Director whispers to Camera Operator:
Servant is smiling at Mrs Japprey's English-
y Indian, plus accent. I hear his rouge moustache
rhymes with his hero – Dennis Rodman's crewcut.
Turn all lights off except the one that's lit
     circling his mouth.

Camera Operator whispers back:
Rumour has it, his sound poem called 'Arsonate'
which if with vowels fully inserted might smart
us all. Is a curse poem! Not some primal 'ursonate'.
Poets will miss this – the servant has a boom
very reminiscent of a proud-chested Punjab
character who's irate in talkie from Pollywood.

*In the darkness, except for his lit mouth, the servant
recites his sound poem loudly*

Arsonate

ouverture					
	brrrr rrr	bbbrshrrr	hmmm brrrbbbr		4
	bndbst	upna bnd	kkkrrrrhhhh rrrr		3
		brrr	bbbrshrrr	rrrr	4
		brrr	bbbrshrrr	rrrr	4
	bqws tmk		kdho qtm	bfkf	5
desarrollo	bnd				1
		bnd			1
		bnd			1
	bdtmz	chungrrrr	rrrrorrrrrrr		5
			pkpkpkpkpk		3
				nung	1
				ggrrrb	1
	mrgggyh	rrrrrrrrrr			3
			ggrrrb		1
			ggrrrb		1
finalis	tuuuuuuuuuuuu kaaaaaaaaaaaah				2
	tuuuuuuuuuuuu kaaaaaaaaaaaah				2

*Poets shout wah!wah! & applaud; lights are back on & the servant
recedes from view; Mrs Japprey's dish is served to each poet*

Mrs Japprey, pleased, replies to her servant:
Tu kaah – you eat. Tickety-boo, servant! Everyone
please, fill your boots. You gasp, dear collectorate –
gasp as each of you hold over your Macaroni pie.
Yes – 'tis a geyser of gravy come squirting up
from a central node in the crust before crust
has even been struck from its contrivance.
What does it infer – there lies my cryptic touch.

Director whispers to Camera Operator:
How Mrs Japprey winks at camera! Every outline

of her wrinkled yet refined skin makes a lyric
of maturity. Her face is modestly magnetic.

CHORUS:
In background, as the servant had turned about
for the kitchen, Ms Homi Bibi, our bampot poet
of high Coolie, & bidi smoking Ms Begum Jaan,
       whose poems had bore a raffish sound,
       both fist-pump the servant! Fist-pump done,
       the servant returns back into the stance,
       the stoop of a garlanded pooja-cow.

   Mr Desani walks over to Director:
Dear chap, by the by, what's this Coolie folderol,
this pig's breakfast, this, this caninum prandium.
Why stage a suitless Coolie, when the indigent
must always appear biddable, forgettable.
Brecht may have advocated plumpes denken, that blunt
thinking is best – we have here an excess raw rent.

   Director shuffles in his shoulder-pads to retort:
When Mrs Japprey delivered her servant at our gate,
he was 420° starkers. He stood before us a grape
of thorns, a fig of thistles. We crowned him, savoir faire,
head to toe in Hush Puppies & raven wig of a film star.

       After a while, the mood of the talkie set seems to be changing
       as brightness increases in the hall

   Camera Operator observes to Director:
Scores of phonetical oddities from our poets
that I have lose correct pronunciation of each consonant.
They have been pronouncing a word such as poem –
pims, perm, prem, psalm, pompom, bomb.
Once for a penny farthing, poem as poem.

Director replies:
Dear Operator, script is mere husk – our folio
could transcribe every time e as ë, ō for o!
Also, you do not say 'poem' as 'poem'
you always say 'poem' as 'param'.

Camera Operator touches the Director's gold nail while laughing

Camera Operator replies:
Param mean supreme, so I am in param sharam!
Of some *indiom* poems, may I ask why poetic forms
have syllable metrics that are found in Indian poems?

Director employs the Thirukurral couplet:
As Blighty verse deploys a cuckoo rendition
of Greek metrics – we'll cuckoo with Indian.

Camera Operator replies:
Yes, Kural's statue is cross-legged on patch of SOAS
lawn. Statues? Let's touch not that blood-boil on Al-
bion's bonce, which foams in its furor teutonicus!

Director whispers to Camera Operator:
Let's also not chew the cud of how, at best, this talkie
is an elite of elite talkie of a talkie critique of critique.

Camera Operator asks:
Much talkie talk has been on panegyre & satire,
is not *indiom* old school satire – polemic, corrective?
Or what tone is best suiting our grinding times?

Director replies:
The philosopher Sir Roger Scruton once discussed how Mr
Joyce compared Leopold Bloom to Ulysses. It's a comparison

that's funny as a banana skin japery; Bloom being a sweaty
fellah while Ulysses has mega-pecs on wits. Sir Roger says
such comparison, 'causes us to laugh at its object only by
laughing at ourselves. It forces upon us a perception of our
own kinship.' I declare such irony is a form of praise, however
slight, it tends less to satire & more to panegyre. It's the sort of
jocular praise that gives salt to a best friend's wedding speech.
Perhaps our age would prefer the emolliatory, eiderdown
warmth of panegyre than satire's wire woolling.

Camera Operator, smiling, says:
Not to umbrage – you have pelted two-times
prose upon me. I am not low caste! Mine noggin
best intersects via the mechanisms of rhyme.
For intercourse with me, please, in poetics!

Director smiles:
indiom has been remiss – even denying villanelle,
sonnet, sestina & every poet's new go-to, ghazal.

CHORUS:
Director & his fellow say, 'Know they Blighty'
          then titter & talee. Then cease mid-
talee having realised the bombshell whammy –
          it's here! Talkie's end!

Everyone cease also their joyous ovation,
as though they entered a thick realisation,
for Ms Homi Bibi & Apache Brummy
who have complete their mandala weave
which they unfold in the Hall like a flag –
laid out, it becomes vast & seems to appear
vertical as horizontal across the talkie screen.

36

Mr Desani's call to action

On affluent British Babus who treat everyone as
mere Coolies, on a bulldog who needs to accept the
British empire is over

☙

CHORUS:
Spotlight is return to our Augustean Chair.
Everyone surprised dénouement is already declare.
Is like greeting a tutting Babu who tut because
no soon he start reading *The Decameron* that al-
ready the thousands page have quickly pass.
So it is, troubadours feel they been in Bulbul Hall
for a mere stitch of time – not Shutup for yonks!

Mr Vishnoodas Desani addresses the poets:
Hail all et cetera! Let's conclude our symposia
that's been side-tracked, cul-de-sac'd with suchlike of ring
    saga,
attention-seeking cricket ball, Pimm's, road signs, & a sharp

tum. Have we laughed, or who has been laughing. Let the
    mimic
not mock his CEO. In the West – boss is a cumin
whiffed migrant who has made good, whose darksome &
    Caucasian

workforce he regard all the same – dinkum Coolie. So who
dare imitate their magnate, a magnate whose Mammon
     swoons
the oil pits of the Gulf. If these profit-only Babus

show English is a dogsbody on Time's leash, that all must
bark to the lines of a magnate – we're doomed! Let our bon
     mots
make invisible insurrections in miles of bonces.

          Camera Operator whispers to Director:
Mr Desani seem not himself. He scratch his garter.
His chat-pace is being in hell for leather.

          Mr Desani continues:
I spied a bulldog 'neath the statue of Cromwell. It wore
the jingo weeds of St George to match his proprietor.
I braved that pup & told it thus, 'a pathologiser

would detect from your staunch – you never experienced
     grief,
as all your colonies busted out like autumnal leaves
you drank sack to blotter the shame. Your manservant, a
     Jeeves,

sweeps off your colonial dew each day. Oh bulldog, who
joi de vivres in yellow garters while you & Jeeves are blue
old sock? Whine not cur, Babu has arrived & cobwebs will
     blow –

          Mr Vishnoodas Desani stops speaking mid-sentence
               because of an interruption

37

Duo Mr Desanis

On who is the real Mr Vishnoodas Desani, & grati-
tude to the technical crew

~

Mr Kumbarkarn is seen by all taking off his own clothes

CHORUS:
Arrey, zounds! Major incident interruptus.
Mr Vishnoodas Desani's snowball
of zaggy rhetoric has hit the tropics of a thaw.
Look over there – the hippopotamusly huge
Mr Kumbarkarn has sudden risen from his roost
in a far-off corner. He's stood amid hellacious
gasping all round. Gasps not for the interruptus
(overtalk is, yes, a sign of bonhomie in the Indus)
but that Mr Kumbarkarn, is well, frankly, is
dispossess himself of his entirety green outfit!

Shocking it is! Mr Kumbarkarn – his every garment
he's stripping off. Below is yellow blazer & crossed
yellow garters. He's even dispossessed
of his facial flesh having picked the raiment
of his skin. His artificial skin clean disposed
so its 'buskin' bulk is lain rubber by his dapper shoes,
like messy waxing strips with hair-side shown.
        With face & fabrics removed
is not Mr Kumbarkarn look the spit, the majest

of our dashing Pendragon. What, what a heck
of happenstance!? Has Mr Vishnoodas been in disguise
from the off, or during Intermission – we can't surmise.

The impersonator of Mr Desani speaks:
Am I Mr Vishnoodas Desani? Or is our magus the one
who ventriloquised through cunnery & sleight to become
Mr Kumbarkarn. Yet in sooth, no cat is ever them

-self except for the synaptical sinews of language
they uniquely haute couture. Can I ever be the whit
of that dashing mask!? If he's creation's own true spirit

I am a mere muse of cow-dung fire. As he is Poo Bah
or Eiffel, I am Tom Thumb. I am Mr Shivnoodas!
Our lord's been liveried as truant, Mr Kumbarkarn.

*Everyone realises that Mr Kumbarkarn is absent, that Mr Desani
has been disguised as Mr Kumbarkarn, that Mr Shivnoodas
has been disguised as Mr Vishnoodas*

Camera Operator whispers to Director:
Mr Vishnoodas been elongating his flaxen tash which had
drooped like the wine legs in a handblown glass. He'd
been pursing his lips, while Mr Shivnoodas just spoke,
to pass him, across the room, the very bell plus whistle
of kisses with final downpour of snog-blow like a sink,
a toy kitchen-sink for kiddies, chucked in.

Director replies:
Divine play of the gods, it is. I endear this fandango
of shape-shifting, impersonating for a preter-folderol.
Emulating a fellow, to their very pigmentation,
helps us appreciate the career of each mortal condition.

Instagram pics & vids on the walls of the room
of Mr Vishnoodas & Mr Shivnoodas in jockstrap
for rural kabbadi, for polo, tug-of-war dishoom,
or serving tapioca to victims of a mishap.
Who could tell apart this Vish from that Shiv?
Is like spotting the exact slim-jim patch of Sherwood
grass where once had forty-winked Mr Hood.
Indeed, who could spot this Shiv from that Vish?

Footage of Mr Vishnoodas & Mr Shivnoodas stops

Mr Shivnoodas addresses the collectorate:
The world is a match too much of us. But now, now by God
before we must arise to head for a bee-glade, before
I wish you all a month of ivories, apes & peacocks,

before we head for Innerpeffray to borrow a book
or the finest festival in the world at Ullapool
or Glasgow women's festival (this year it's digital) –

let's not forget to applaud our personal Orson Welle.
The Director & his team who have framed us in welters
of blockbuster angle. Be seen for once, dear Director!

Director whispers to Camera Operator:
I will adopt modesty & creep out
to receive my undeserved hullabaloo,
but come, you must all join me – come also camera crew,
let us all take our bow.

*Camera crew & the Director stand near the main table
to receive their applause*

Camera Operator whispers to Director:
Mr Vishnoodas is creep-up to put his arms round
both our waist! He's lifting us lofty off the ground!

Director replies:
He's so brawny & we are a tad chubster.
He must feel as though he's plucked up
two bodies bulgy as a puffball fungus.

Camera Operator, smiling, whispers:
Recall, dear Director, I am not a male,
please desist on us your lingo of toxic gaze.

*Director & Camera Operator are in the air, one in each arm
of Mr Vishnoodas Desani, & take turns speaking to each other,
saying the final sentence, below, together*

Director & Camera Operator whisper:
Ooh he's so Lancelot – he's a full Bull Assyrian!
Ooh he's so Adamantean – he's Samsonian!
He's a thunking scrum-gargantua
samosa packed Samoan!

*Director & camera crew are placed on the ground & walk backwards,
stooped, back to their positions*

CHORUS:
Mr Shivnoodas is about to extemporise, to springboard
but what – a sound is heard over Hall, like loud sticker
being pulled off the page. It feel *tickly* but is no sticker,
is yellow tape from every red brick & ornate wood
being undressed because Populous Shutup is pass.
The Bulbul Hall of Charsovee bestow discharge,
emancipation for elbow room, utter azaaaaad!

CANTO

IV½

38

Duo Apus

On a confrontation between Satyajit Ray's Apu from
Pather Panchali & Apu from *The Simpsons*

〜

As if by magic, two Apus appear on the set & confront each other

CHORUS:
Committee seem scared to inhale the outdoor contagion,
some don masks. Forming before all – a double phantom
comes alive in the Hall! Flesh or filmic? One is *Simpsons'*
Apu in colour, he stands by – it's Satyajit Ray's film
hero, the child, Apu, in black & white. The two Apus
stare knowingly at each other, in a father-to-son
or hero-to-traitor style. Mr Shivnoodas is pull
himself between them. A magnetic force has crashed
him backward to a wall by the reins of his wide moustache!
To repeat the miracle, Ray's Apu's in black & white,
he's dwarfed by *Simpsons'* Apu – a gaudy adult.

Simpsons' Apu says to Ray's Apu:
What's in a name, dear suckling? It's a word
a wolf may blow down if the piggery's unfirm.
But if a name occupies you, why, name's a game!
I was cast in a curious house. From my brown store,
whatsoever I said or dumb-showed – I shuffled all
mortal-coils into LOLs. I was honey-potted to stardom
with no say over being role-model or racist bum.
Yes, I admit that I was named after Peter Sellers'

monkey. The monkey, it's true, was named after
you. You are my mock-star of Bethlehem, Apu.

Camera Operator whispers to Director:
Simpson Apu is speak slow & dry, not super-high
Babu as normal. He wear shades which excite
a glam-glow about him, albeit his lips jut
making of his face a platypus cum duck.

Director replies:
Zoom-in at the steps of *Simpsons'* Apu. They're loud!
His high-heeled orthopaedic boot clanks on wood
as he nears next to Satyajit Ray's Apu. He's holding
out for the child a cheap stick of candy. The suckling
has countless wounds across his flesh –
he must bear the wounds of Jesu.

Camera Operator:
If I can intimate. They may be laugh lines,
little wrinkles & cuts provoked on his sweaty
frame where no band-aid will stay skin-tight.
Ray Apu is going up past a chair. Oh dearie!

Director:
He does realise, this is an Escher-style palatial?
He doesn't. His shoeless feet have been caught
in a snag, he's fallen by the boots of his namesake.
Can he lift himself by his own brawn? He can't!

Camera Operator:
Blighted infant. Ray Apu is splatter on the floor
by the candy. He's about to speak in Bengali,
he's still black & white staring up at the superstar
from over the pond. Ray's Apu's brittle as the candy!

Director whispers:
I assume your auntie from Sunderland has writ
the subtitles, albeit English is not her strong suit!

Satyajit Ray's Apu speaks:
Am I look monkey-esque? Or 'A Poo'? Your candy, it
yours. Regard me exotic? By so doing, you denied
face-to-face of what in me you scared. You laugh out of
me instead. Embodying me, you have leave me calcified
to my bare eyes. One bite of your candy & I turn blot.

Director whispers to Camera Operator:
Keep close your cameras on Ray's Apu – the stiff joints
of that poor kid from the assault of global laughout.
He feels the whole world has poked at his name
after Peter Sellers sought to mock Satyajit Ray.

Camera Operator replies:
Having meet *Simpson* Apu, his mission is been famished.
His dry cough – it float a morsel of blood the screen catch.

Director replies:
His eyes have gone Miltonic – milling eyeless-in-Gaza grey.
He's to recite in the Salve genre which is ideal for making
a salutation. He's readying with a fading arm upraised.

39

Death & afterlife

On pleading for salvation, & a tragic death

◆

Ray Apu recites his Salve faintly, from the centre of Bulbul Hall

Lord, Julian of Norwich say Jesu'
blood
run like rain off la maison from heavy
     pour.
So much blood – each drop pour for each of his
        flock.
Yet blood of whole world is rise to skin
        flooded
with ridicule in my name. Uncheek this
        scorn
worse than wound! Oh place me at your top
        table.
I too have cause deluge – stare at me your
        face.

From the floor, Ray's Apu is heard making a cry

   Director whispers to Camera Operator:
He makes a fatal cry, so feeble
is hardly screen-detectable
yet it is sickly powerful.

Camera Operator replies:
I'm contemplating Agamemnon by Aeschylus;
struck me it has – that boy's salve is like cry
from Cassandra which shock Mrs Woolf to write,
Cassandra's cry 'exploded on striking mine ears'
I think the sound was as follows – oi hoitoitoitoieeee!!!

Director:
All are observing the boy's orbs, those twin engines
destined to act a wretched character part on terrain.
        They have now shut down.

Camera Operator:
Ray Apu's unused passport is fall from his pocket.
        His neck is now relax hardfast.
        Dead he is! Dead by the cartoon's
        orthopaedic space foot.

CHORUS:
A pure rare silence has been entering the room.
As a forest is gnarled by one mere Hanuman breath,
so the air's rarefied. Then a god floats through
before Ray's Apu. The poets have all been wrenched
back to the room's fringes – sprawled in its dips,
its elevations! What is the playfulness of all this?
In the oofy light, brighter than even the camera crew,
is this god, Jesu? No! Muhammadan or Hindu guru?

Director whispers to Camera Operator:
What? I hear in my ear it's a god from *Star Trek* fame!
It's – what? It's the Borg Queen! No vanilla Borg Queen,
instead she's peat-bog bodied, fluorescent green by face.

Camera Operator replies:
We're capturing her essence – her gorgeous gothic.
Beads about her neck, her dress in Phoenician fretwork.
Is said the Borg cogito's so hot it even make suck
Babus – for they suck rival minds into their brainbox.

CHORUS:
The Borg Queen stands over the child & straights
his dead body, the way a burial mother might stroke
a child's wrinkles to clear the final hurt. Two raised
fingers she is tapping on the child's cheeks. His face,
eek, is peeling away from his head like a, a mask!

She steers Ray Apu's face toward herself, it's risen
golden! Like Duchy egg – is carried to celluloid heaven.
To celluloid heaven for the Hall of Fame!
Does his nemesis, Peter Sellers, inhabit the selfsame?

Troubadours have remained stagger-shocked.
Some are nudging a near-laid fellow, 'Look how in moht,
Apu was grinned.' 'The dead boy will stay in corporeal
humour.' It seems that when Ms Borg Queen appealed
for Ray Apu's face, as it made exit from his head,
a chin-tickle left Apu with a post-moht giggle effect
hinted across the remnant veneer of his facial.

This miracle seems to have been missed by our heroic
Apu of *Simpsons*. He nubs a finger on his cheek,
what has he caught? A tear, teeer! His first human tear.
He beats his chest, wild-weeping, but no sound is rear
its head! He starts to vanish like world of silent talkie.

Both Apus have disappeared & the poets prepare to leave the workshop

40

Poets leave Bulbul Hall

On poets being chased out of Bulbul Hall, & a revela-
tion about the true nature of the Hall

Director & the Camera Operator are walking for the exit door

Director says to Camera Operator:
Pulley the curtains in – this talkie is finito.

Camera Operator replies:
No poet wanting to leave by physical
or virtual door, then sudden they all
go screaming off the roof now scrammed
to escape downhill! But what is cause
our troubadours fall in forward rolls
& helter-skelter? A battle, or attack?
By what do we Indian lose our bottle?

Director appears to know all & replies:
First, I tell you why we are being bombarded.
The air in Bulbul Hall's been ripening with odours,
the vowels of civilisations been brewing flavours
like a smell from Macaroni pies so concentrated
their juicing the environment to make demented
our foe who, en masse, has yapping slipped-in.
Who'd not lick the air's very fruity lips!
Follow me & see why our poets are tormented.

Director & Camera Operator are out of the Hall & running downhill
behind the puppy poodles who are chasing the terrified poets

Camera Operator to Director:
Gnash on the Ogden 'Nasher' couplets – the exodus
require Babu brio! I follow after you, my dear Pegasus.

Director replies:
To be descrying it, hearing it – there's a crèche-load
of Charsovee poodles who've rioted our abodement

terrifying our troubadours who've from the Hall skedaddled;
notwithstanding a prince in Mahabharat, on his packsaddle,

as it were, would take to heaven his beloved bow wow
or he'd rather be hellbound! Who did that pow wow

from the epic inspire? None. All Indians would pick
damnation than chien! Particularly now that the monadnock

which our poets run down has behind them an infantry
of gharam-breath poodles charged like the Indic Red Ea-

gle Division that crucified the Axis thus ending the North
African campaign. These uncanny, these teeny behemoth

giving chase are arranged in flanks of sepoy cockapoo,
of schnoodle, poochon, of poma- puga- Yorki- poo!

In rows, the 25-pounder bark of westipoo, sproodle,
& canon-fodder jackapoo, cavapoo, whoodle!

Our poets are downward bound, shouting bejesus-scared,
I quote, 'each newborn have throat loaded-with-bear

like the Cyclop lair', 'every tongue it's the Voldemort
Naaagini', 'hair like fakir's nailbed', 'bite of Morlock',

another troubadour hollering down the monadnock,
'pup's making like Whitman's feral yawp from the rooftop

of the world!' 'stay-sit-sit-argh!' The Raj needn't be bygone
if Viceroy had subdued the subaltern with our Room 101 –

chien. If chien were commissioned for the Khyber Pass,
the Mutiny, the Black Hole of Calcutta – every khyber pass

of every subaltern would have burst their khaki
shorts, & every Babu'd still be cleansing for monarchy.

Let's conclude these Nashers which show us as befkoof
who starve chien then fear 'em, never breaking the oofta

cycle! Let's conclude with a shocking beguilement
at how our traumatised poets leave the subcontinent.

Unlike some dream of Scipio poem, our downhillers
curry-burp, then flagging – they appear hebetudinous.

On the plain now they go slow, slow as though on the spot,
halted. Then all are – will-o'-the-wisp – gone AWOL!

Truly, our troubadours vanished with the breakneck
of Lord Mountbatten & his two-month high-tech

cartographers who came, who saw, who divided
(for Partition-Kashmir-Liberation War) Ind.

But gone? While running on a level across theatre boards!?
Yes, on theatre boards. Not down Charsovee! Troubadours

fantoosh vanished, as though inside the leopard-suave
PVC art folder the Screenwriter on stage leave; one baal –

hair – one vantablack poodle baal wuthering aside the suave
up-standing folder whose mouth stands open. As bizarre

an alternative – could poets have recited their hometime's
poem, in a popty-ping pinged to their condominiums!?

*Poets have gone, Director has stopped running & seems to be
on a stage instead of down a hill*

Director concludes:
Perhaps our 'Indian' audience needs to ask –
was dog scene a test? If they have laughed
are they ashamed of us? If they've kindled
offence – are you the canny Woke kind?

Camera Operator replies:
I finally caught you up! You're a nippy Seb Coe.
But now. It seem we're on own chappal straps, alone.
No poets present at the talkie.
Plus we're not down a hill.
Is seem whole plantation of furniture, fitting
& farrago, even Bulbul Hall itself, is like a flat-
pack & packed away in a burgundy & thin
art folder that might also house a Beatus Map.
Safe to predict, all spectacle is sans rendered
bereft excepting these bare-white theatre board.

Director & Camera Operator pace about the stage enjoying the solitude

Camera Operator, boldly, to Director:
No whispering requisite, we are stardom-staged centre!
Shall I? I shall, yes, perform my first flight in verse.

Before a camera, in the Spanish octastitch, the Huitan
for my hippeydonian ideals. Oh please be indulgence.

Camera Operator clears his throat then recites:
When youngster I was, in Blighty, no words
knew I of English. Yet I much endear
comedy on telly – how all laugh hard
in audience or voiceover. I hear
all Blighty, as one, at jokes, full of chuff!
What a gullible or fight-through-own-spats
populace! I laugh to learn is canned-laugh.
May all humans one day can-laugh madcap!?

Director, clapping, replies:
A lay in the medium Babu. I wish you
one day the gold-standard – high Babu!

Camera Operator, nervously:
I, I have sign-up for a poetry workshop
to juggernaut my style. Is in Village of Twin.
In Kerala. May you too, perhaps – come along?

CHORUS:
Camera Operator go colour of aubergine sat
on a veg stall; say our Director is customer –
will customer take shining brinjal to hand
then swoop in brown bag this Special Offer?
Director pause, look at theatre lights,
then his face slow-holee-holee turn bright!
Bright as brinjal – it does seem he will buy.

Director replies to Camera Operator:
Shabash plan, chum-mahee. Let's conjoin Screenwriter
Companion with us hither for our next talkie thither.

Director & Camera Operator are walking down the steps of the stage,
Camera Operator is seen happily tapping the three cards in his back pocket

Camera Operator:
Perhaps she's with the Screenwriter in a pavilion.
Plus, we never hear Miss Pushpa T.S., her verdict
on Nissim poem, on Babuism, on our entire talkie action.

CHORUS:
We are in chockful bankside quietude
reminiscent of Greek skene, Green Room,
where theatre plus its rear are indistinguishable
so that removed-stage & hillside commingle.

Where we are is contrary to discern – outdoors, yet
indoors are we? On Mother Earth or in heavenly?

A far off shadowplay, Mr E. M. Forster's in tonga
for Ujjain near River Shipra, oh – his arms
aloft at site ancient as Rome, where his hero poet
dreamt for his rasa essences, the ancient Kalidasa.

If one were to dekko, one could discern thousand
such homecoming. Though soon all is diminished.
Everywhere now is horizonless bloom-bucolic.

Yet every good petal to frond know Babu's no chum
of lyric time – not pertaining to continuum shtum.
Multiple ending, regenerativity, is indiom decorum.
Even Babu cannot resist
the arrival of toodle pip.

41

Epilogue by Screenwriter

EPILOGUE offering gratitude to the audience

A figure stands near their PVC art folder

CHORUS:
Who is in bouffant & kameez, plus sandals
with hands clasped to hover though mist into view;
it is, yes, your Screenwriter! Their hair wear pearl –
     their skin cosmic blue.

Screenwriter recites a Sapphic ode

Dear talkie fandom, how kind you stayed in seat!
It's true, I sought the advice of Rosalind,
you know them from *As You Like It*, on how best
     to kaput our rhyme.

They was cross-dress & leaned against a greenwood
at the forest of Arden – where else! They stroke
my brows then say, 'always keep fandom in mind –
     they'll gatekeep your jokes'.

Dear fandom, we passed the Marmite Test, yes/no?
Did you feel ink-throated by too-much lightness,
if yes, please – what should we change? We aim to blow
     wet chumchum kisses.

Now, what else is it dreamy Rosalind say,
'if you enjoy indioms – know that you too
are a thespian. So would you not create
        work that creates you.'

What's that dear viewer? You would strut your Babu
nothings on the boards with me & Rosalind.
But when you ride our tongue – you become the beau
        floodlit at our side.

If you should long for our touch, why – we are here
at lip with the smile you smile each day, & verse
updates over time – so who's the one been near
        at lip unobserved?

This whole year, we've observed each other at play.
But what!? Our time is up! Our fun must depart!?
Let me air-kiss all you stars with namaste
        plus crore au revoir.

FINIS

42

Outtake featuring Ms Gussama Beenon

OUTTAKE on falling in love with the English language after first hearing a word spoken in English

Part of the way through Scene 20, while poets are composing a poem inspired by Hobson-Jobson Hanklyn-Janklin, Ms Gussama Beenon, of the two rutputty homes, tells Mr Common Man a story

Mr Common Man is heard saying:
So the tale you'll digress me with's in naani metrics.
        I appreciate its syllabics, is used for 'sole
leading to whole'.

Ms Gussama Beenon adds:
Naani is used to give human cohabitation a thumb
        up for its good relations. I may have mucked
naani syllables a tad but it feels better for English,
        for when I tell of a new word back in
1944 that filled the public eardrums.

Poets who were playing the Hobson-Jobson Hanklyn-Janklin game have stopped to hear Ms Gussama Beenon's story

Ms Gussama Beenon says:
I'll recite now this tale which is from my pigtail silly
        days. Once, over breakfast,
my great-grandfather, a Babu – was reading a broadsheet
        when he shout, *eureka!*

He's impressed by a word, in an article, just devised,
    by a Polish lawyer.
'Whole damn shooting match of history is here summarised',
    says my great-grandfather.

He speak Punjabi at home, yet keep repeating this word
    in English, 'So small, yet
gobful. One sound that's been built to characterise the world.'
    The office in my head

held that word from a tongue I never heard before. A strange
    language – I'd earn as mine!
I'd shakti me with the music giving British sahibs
    their grand Herculean

lexicality! In my 'office', I'd conduct the strain
    great-grandfather cited.
I sung its first sound – its opening j that made the cave
    of my mouth touch inside

as it tumbled into the en – the pathos of its o –
    its c-sea – its i-eye
held under by that firmed d. On my swing, I swung high-low
    to the piecemeal I'd chime.

    toom mera junnaside lokoya heh
    you have hidden my junnaside

    koini rokh sadda mera Jinnasyde
    no one can stop my Jinnasyde

    mera sareer heh Joonasyde kah
    my body belongs to Joonasyde

tum mera Jeevan heh, Jernasyde
you are my life – my love, Jernasyde

Ms Gussama Beenon looks nervous, she is pressing a palm against
the Faber paperback edition of indiom, *with its Berthold Wolpe*
typeface, which is rested on her lap

In class one day, I say to Sir, 'though I will stop learning,
      stop to wed – my marriage
will be with English.' Sir have a clove-shapen head. His burn,
      'Girls, girls befriend English!?'

'I'll make all words my befriend – some already have a haunt
      in me.' I rush to tell
who is my beloved – 'Jernosyde.' 'What!?', he say. 'Jennis-
      yde, Sir. Junnasyd. Jen –'

'Befkoof! Shut it up,' he say, 'scold your tongue in turmeric
      before I put your head
whole-stock in Wagga Wagga Oil to loosen its fooldom!'
      He say, 'It's a cruel word

whose sense turns ears to run blind within even a mirror.'
      Wet-eyed, he say, 'Stand by
me – on one leg.' Of 'genocide', he repeat its horror
      & watch me puke. That night

I sleepwalk for our garden, & lay in a garden hole.
      Dear Mr Common Man,
to this day – what holds us but humour. I stretch out myself
      from pigtail to chappal

to bear for the world, from all sides, the heft of what was
   meant
      by that deceptive strain.

The fragrance of rue & fennel drew my corpus afloat
 till I sung human pain.

By lying there, I took from my mouth what was crafted
 for my tum. If I nudge
by just a knuckle – veins of language would empty my blood.
 In my hole, I'd bear the cost

 of all what is loved & lost.

Acknowledgeability

Cast of *indiom* would seek to lick kulfis of kindness for the British Empire most especially the bodacious Raj; in addition, a debt of humility to Faber's crack squad of Sahib Matthew Hollis – very superlative editor – Memsahibs Lavinia Singer, Jane Feaver & Arabella Watkiss, also plus Sahib Hamish Ironside being a typesetter of utmost invention; not being remiss to recall readers of first draft poet-Sahibs Edward Doegar & Richard Scott; most uncommonly, a heap of affection is flower-showering over daughters Hannah, Maia & Escha (inc. son-in-law, Anish), but most chiefly also to mehaboob, being Rani Katherine who has read, advised & persevered with many pertinent hearings while always remaining in generous cheer, a most beautiful soulmate on the all-mannered journey; not forgetting guinea pigs Bobby & Custard remaining equal to that eminently kissable jack-apoo, Jago; while also saluting Memsahib Imtiaz Dharker for permitting a fancy upon the Duo Dharkers, albeit the construction within these papers was based on a lost interview with Nissim Ezekiel, of whom, what would this talkie be without, were it not for his shabash of all Babu poems, *Goodbye Party for Miss Pushpa T.S.* for which *indiom*, while also adoring Sahib G. V. Desani, is but a meagre thanking-you party conducted in a time of viral embroilment.